Anita Shackelford

Surface Textures

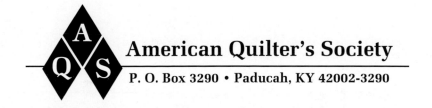

American Quilter's Society

P. O. Box 3290 • Paducah, KY 42002-3290

Located in Paducah, Kentucky, the American Quilter's Society (AQS), is dedicated to promoting the accomplishments of today's quilters. Through its publications and events, AQS strives to honor today's quiltmakers and their work – and inspire future creativity and innovation in quiltmaking.

EXECUTIVE EDITOR: JANE R. MCCAULEY
BOOK DESIGN: WHITNEY L. HOPKINS
ILLUSTRATIONS: ELAINE WILSON
COVER: KAREN CHILES
TECHNICAL EDITOR: BONNIE K. BROWNING
PHOTOGRAPHY: CHARLES R. LYNCH

Library of Congress Cataloging-in-Publication Data

Shackelford, Anita.
    Surface textures / Anita Shackelford.
       p. cm.
    Includes bibliographical references (p. 134).
    ISBN 0-89145-890-5
    1. Trapunto. 2. Trapunto--Patterns. 3. Quilting. 4. Quilting-
-Patterns. 5. Texture (art)   Title.
    TT835.S4626   1997
    746.46--dc21   97-1123
                                               CIP

Additional copies of this book may be ordered from: American Quilter's Society,
P.O. Box 3290, Paducah, KY 42002-3290 @ $24.95. Add $2.00 for postage & handling.

Copyright: 1997, Anita Shackelford

ACKNOWLEDGMENTS

Many people have made significant contributions to this book. I am fortunate and grateful to have the support and encouragement of a loving family and many friends who have shared their time, their knowledge, and their beautiful quilts with me. To all, I say "Thank You."

To my husband, Richard, and my daughters, Jennifer and Elisa, for giving me the time to study, to create, and to share my work with others for so many years. These quilts are for you.

To my aunt, Virginia Reiff, for instilling in me a love of antique quilts.

To a very special group of quiltmakers: Glenda Clark, Janet Hamilton, Ruth Kennedy, Sheila Kennedy, Jo Lischynski, Joan Longbrake, Connie St. Clair, and Rebecca Whetstone for their encouragement and friendship and for always being ready to accept the next challenge.

To friends and fellow American Quilt Study Group members Barbara Brackman, Sara Dillow, Joyce Gross, Nancy Hornback, Ardis and Robert James, Fumie Ono, Bets Ramsey, Terry Clothier Thompson, and Merikay Waldvogel for sharing their knowledge, their photos, and quilts from their collections.

To Kathryn Berenson for her meticulous study of the history of *broderie de Marseille* and her generosity in sharing her findings and her beautiful Marseilles quilts.

To Stearns Technical Textiles Co. for sharing a wonderful trapunto quilt from the Mountain Mist collection.

To the Baltimore Museum of Art, The Saint Louis Art Museum, the Museum of the American Quilter's Society, and the National Museum of History for understanding the importance of caring for and sharing these important textiles.

To Irma Gail Hatcher, Jane Holihan, Debra Wagner, Beverly Mannisto Williams, and others working in this style, for adding so much to this tradition.

To Bill and Meredith Schroeder for their continuing support of the art of quiltmaking and for giving me the opportunity to share my work in so many ways.

To my editor and good friend, Bonnie Browning, for her unfailing support and for bringing all of the pieces of this book together.

To Whitney Hopkins for her computer expertise in laying out the book, and to Elaine Wilson for drawing the illustrations.

To photographer, Charles R. Lynch, for his skill in capturing this beautiful work on film.

CONTENTS

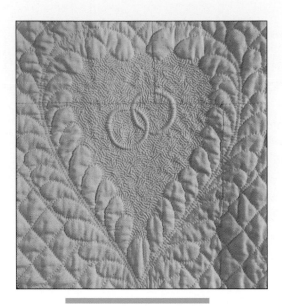

INTRODUCTION

My love affair with quilts has been a long one. I have always been intrigued by the look and feel of quilts, their heavy softness, the placing of pattern against pattern, and especially by the wonderful texture of a piece of cloth which has been layered with a soft inner lining and quilted through.

I have been making quilts for nearly thirty years, working in a variety of styles from piecing to appliqué, to whole cloth. The quilting designs have always held a special fascination for me. After the quilt top is finished, the next, equally important, design challenge is to create a quilting pattern which will complement the main surface design and please the eye.

When I included corded work and stipple quilting in two small areas of a quilt in 1985, I had not actually seen any of this type of work "in person."

Since that time, my interest in antique quilts has included a study of raised work, both corded and stuffed, in whole cloth quilts or in combination with patchwork or appliqué. In studying the raised

work on these early quilts and experimenting with the technique, I began looking for a way to add this beautiful texture to my own quilts without causing damage to the quilt. Working from the inside rather than through the top or the back of the quilt seems to solve this problem.

I use three different techniques when adding raised work to my quilts and garments. Depending on the design and the desired effect, the areas may be corded, padded, or stuffed. All of these different approaches to the work can be done behind the top layer, before it is prepared for quilting.

When I write about techniques used in antique quilts, I feel that it is important to include some of the history of the subject, to show how or where it began, and to tie the technique to its roots.

I am indebted to those quilt historians who have researched the subject of Marseilles quilts and other raised work and am pleased to share a small portion of that information here. The bibliography will lead you to resources for further study.

While experimenting with the process of adding raised work to a quilt top, I have tried to cover a number of variations in technique, design style, and approaches to the work and to present several options.

The technique section of the book includes small blocks with explanations of each technique, meant to be used as step-by-step samples, and to guide you through the individual approaches to the work. In the back of the book, you will find a large pattern section with blocks which can be used in combination with patchwork or appliqué, or set together in a whole cloth style. Each pattern page includes specific notations to suggest which technique should be used to develop the surface texture in each motif. Some of these patterns might also be translated into appliqué, either flat or dimensional.

A study of background quilting patterns is also included. Quilting is presented in combination with the raised work, because I feel that the two techniques are inseparable. Fine quilting will recess the background and show raised work to its best effect. You will find various approaches and thoughts on planning a quilting design which will best complement the main surface elements of the quilt, plus the techniques to achieve the desired effect.

Throughout the book you will find quilts from museums and private collections which show a wide variety of quilt styles and also the time span of this beautiful work. Other applications or variations of these techniques include garment embellishment and machine work. Everyone working with textiles today should find inspiration here and be tempted to add some form of surface texture to his/her work.

CHAPTER 1

HISTORY OF RAISED WORK

HISTORY OF RAISED WORK

Early references to raised work generally used the term "stuffed work" or "trapunto." Webster's dictionary defines trapunto as "a decorative quilted design in high relief worked through at least two layers of cloth by outlining the design in running stitch and padding it from the underside." Working within this definition, we can find several ways of adding raised work to cloth.

Traditionally, corded work was done by quilting together two layers of fabric. Quilted channels were then filled with a cotton cording to create raised patterns. Yarn was inserted from the wrong side of the quilt, often causing damage and leaving the ends of the yarn exposed (Plate 1-1).

In addition to cording, cotton stuffing was also used to add rounded dimension to floral, fruit, or feather motifs. The two layers of fabric were quilted together first, with or without batting in between, and stuffing was put into place by separating threads or cutting a small hole in the quilt lining. Antique quilts almost always show some damage or weakening of the fabric from this process (Plate 1-2).

The earliest known quilts in this style are attributed to Sicily c. 1395, and portray the story of Tristram in both corded and stuffed work. One of these quilts is in the collection of the Victoria and Albert Museum in London, one is in the Bargello in Florence, and a third is in a private collection. The quilts are made of two layers of heavy linen quilted with a running stitch in a heavy brown linen thread. Each block tells a story with the figures of knights, kings, horses, ships, castles, and lettering worked in incredibly fine detail. According to Averil Colby, the large quilted patterns were raised with cotton padding and smaller details were quilted after the padding was done.

Many of the early corded and stuffed quilts which made their way into trade with Europe and the American colonies came from the seaport town of Marseilles in the Provence region of France. By the seventeenth century, this popular style of work was being produced in great numbers by quiltmakers in Marseilles, both for domestic use and for export. These whole cloth, corded, and stuffed quilts were commonly referred to by their place of origin as *broderie de Marseille* or Marseilles embroidery.

Whether corded or stuffed, many of these Marseilles quilts had designs so tightly interlaced as to fill the entire ground. This detail photo (Plate 1-3) shows a portion of a Chauffoir, or small throw, with floral designs, worked in corded *broderie de Marseille*. The raised design is developed entirely with corded channels. The quilt has no batting, and the background areas are not quilted. Exquisite

△ **Plate 1-1.** *Marseilles quilt from the wrong side showing exposed tails of yarn. Collection of Fumie Ono, Granada Hills, California. Photo by Anita Shackelford.*

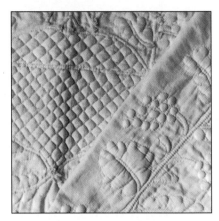

△ **Plate 1-2.** *Corded and stuffed pillow sham, c. 1800– 1840. Collection of Barbara Brackman, Lawrence, Kansas.*

△ **Plate 1-3.** Chauffoir en corded broderie de Marseille, c. 1700, 27" x 32". Collection of Kathryn Berenson, Washington, DC.

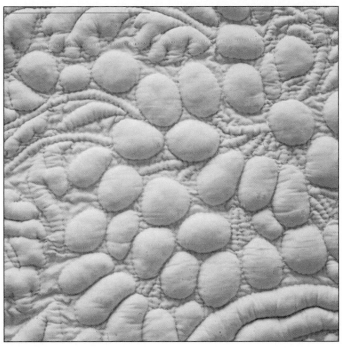

△ **Plate 1-4.** *Detail of grapes from stuffed* broderie de Marseille *bedcover, c. 1825. Collection of Kathryn Berenson.*

△ **Plate 1-5.** *Detail of pineapples or artichokes from stuffed* broderie de Marseille *bedcover, c. 1825. Collection of Kathryn Berenson.*

pieces such as this were made by professional needleworkers primarily for export to royal houses in Spain, Portugal, Holland, Italy, and England.

Detail photos (Plates 1-4 and 1-5) show the beauty and elegance of heavily stuffed fruit motifs combined with corded background fill. Pineapple and grape motifs were used in Provencal needlework from the early eighteenth century.

Another eighteenth century corded *broderie de Marseille* bedcover from the Provence region, includes raised motifs which are further embellished with French knots, adding both texture and detail to the design (Plate 1-6).

The women of Provence added corded and stuffed work to items other than bed covers, including quilted and corded petticoats, camisoles, capes, and bonnets. Layette pieces made for babies included shirts, caps, small lap pads, and crib quilts.

△ **Plate 1-6.** Detail of "Broderie de Marseille" *quilt, embellished with French knots. Collection of Kathryn Berenson*

This all-white corded infant layette piece (Plate 1-7) is from the Provence region c. 1850. Quilted lap pads were used at christenings and other social occasions to protect ladies' fine gowns. These little pieces were made by quilting together two layers of fine cotton in a very close pattern of channels. No batting layer was used. After the piece was quilted, every channel was corded, leaving no background space unfilled.

Designs on early Marseilles quilts are described by Kathryn Berenson as "intermeshed design motifs incorporating highly stylized versions of fauna and flora." A beautiful example of a complex design style can be seen in this corded and stuffed *broderie de Marseille* wedding quilt (Plate 1-8). The elaborate border contains an altar with two flaming hearts, a vase of flowers, two birds in a nest, a young woman in a laced corset, a coquecigrue or mythical figure like a dog with the tail of a fish, a peacock, and two horns of plenty. The background areas are closely filled with undulating leaves and flowers.

In most Marseilles quilts, the cording and stuffing was done with white cotton, although, occasionally indigo dyed cording was used for a color contrast, as shown in this small quilt in Plate 1-9, page 11. The white center of the quilt was originally part of a man's garment. All of the quilting in this area was done with a backstitch rather than a running stitch. In the early 1800's, the piece was recut and borders were added. The cord-

△ **Plate 1-7.** *Infant layette piece, c. 1850, 17½" x 18". Collection of Kathryn Berenson.*

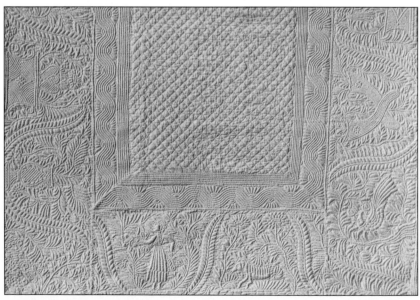

△ **Plate 1-8.** *"Couverture de Mariage," c. 1770–1800, 36" x 47". Collection of Kathryn Berenson.*

△ *Plate 1-9. Corded Marseilles quilt with both white and indigo-dyed yarns, c. 1775–1800, 43" x 53". Collection of Fumie Ono. Photo by Jack Matheison.*

△ *Plate 1-10. Detail from "Hanging Gardens" c. 1835, New England. Mountain Mist Collection.*

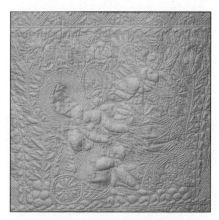

△ *Plate 1-11. New England Whitework, 1815–16, 112½" x 102". Collection of Ardis and Robert James, Chappaqua, New York.*

ing along the joining seams and in the border motifs was done with an indigo dyed cotton yarn, which produces a shadow effect in these areas.

Raised work in the United States was most popular during the period from 1800–1860, with the early work being white, whole cloth quilts. Many of these quilts repeated the Classic style of central medallions, baskets, wreaths, and swags of feathers and fruit.

Typical of the early nineteenth century, the central medallion of a New England quilt features a cornucopia of leaves and flowers, framed with feather swags (Plate 1-10). In another, the majority of the detail work is included in a large, elaborately worked border. The close-up photo shows a woman in a carriage with birds pulling on the reigns and an angel guiding her way (Plate 1-11). On each side are hints of traditional lyre and eagle designs. Leaf and floral designs completely surround the main figures. There is no background quilting in this piece.

Another impressive combination of corded and stuffed work features a large center medallion of flowers, fruits, leaves, and branches surrounded by a Quaker feather wreath (Plate 1-12, page 12). Blossoms and feathers fill the corners and a serpentine feather border frames the piece. The background quilting is worked in closely spaced parallel lines.

A bride's quilt dated 1868 features a symmetrical arrangement of feather wreaths and other running or undulating feathers (Plate 1-13). The heavily stuffed feathers are made even more pronounced by the deeply recessed vein line and the fine background quilting.

White work or raised work was also used in combination with other fabrics and in various styles of quiltmaking throughout the nineteenth century.

One important early quilt features a printed medallion center, with a flower-filled urn surrounded by birds and butterflies, attributed to John Hewson of Philadelphia (Plate 1-14, page 13). Hewson is considered to have been America's foremost printer of textiles in the late eighteenth and early nineteenth centuries. Background areas of the center panel and both white borders are embellished with corded and stuffed work in feather, fruit, and flower designs.

Chintz appliqué was a popular style of quiltmaking during the early nineteenth century. The "Tree of Life" quilt (Plate 1-15, page 14) made by Elizabeth Stouffer in 1809 is a rare and beautiful example of chintz appliqué combined with stuffed and corded work. The heavily stuffed motifs in the border are pushed into high relief by the finely quilted background.

During the mid-nineteenth century, raised work was often used in combination with patchwork or appliqué. Perhaps these are the quilts with which we are most familiar, with raised work used to fill alternate plain blocks or as background detail.

△ *Plate 1-12. Trapunto Whitework, 92" x 90". Collection of Ardis and Robert James.*

△ *Plate 1-13. "Bride's Quilt," 86" x 94" made by Eliza G. Clark, Dale, Indiana, 1868. Collection of Ardis and Robert James.*

△ **Plate 1-14.** *Corded and stuffed work were used in combination with early printed fabrics in this pieced medallion style quilt.*
Center Medallion Quilt, American, c. 1809. Fabric attributed to John Hewson, active 1773–1810. Pieced and appliquéd cotton, quilted. 119" x 115". The St. Louis Art Museum. Purchase. 61:1498.

△ *Plate 1-15.* Raised work and fine background quilting are beautiful additions to this early chintz appliqué quilt. "Tree of Life" Chintz Appliqué, 1809, 107" x 106¾". The Baltimore Museum of Art; gift of William L. Reed, Lutherville, MD, in memory of Barbara Garrett Reed, BMA 1982.140.

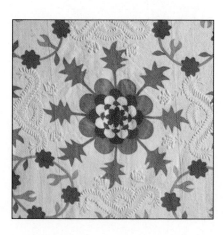

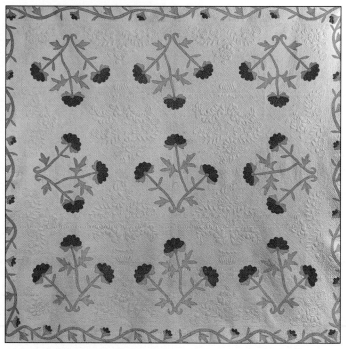

◁ *Plate 1-16. Feathered Star, Pennsylvania, c. 1858, 90" x 90". Collection of Ardis and Robert James.*

△ *Plate 1-17. Floral Appliqué with Stuffed Work, 81" x 84". Collection of the author.*

◁ *Plate 1-18. "Sarah Pollock Quilt," 81" x 82", made by Sarah A. Forsythe Pollock, Ohio 1840-1850. Collection of Paula McFarland. Photo by Jim Meyer, courtesy of Nancy Hornback.*

An 1858 Feathered Star quilt (Plate 1-16) shows a change to the repeated block style of quiltmaking which began in the first half of the nineteenth century and is still popular today. Pieced star blocks alternate with stuffed feather wreaths and are framed with a running feather border. The raised work includes corded veins or spines and stuffed-work feathers. The star blocks are quilted with straight lines spaced ¼" apart and the background behind the wreaths is stipple quilted.

Red and green floral appliqué quilts, so popular in the mid-nineteenth century, provide us with good examples of appliqué combined with stuffed work. In the first example (Plate 1-17), nine floral appliqué blocks are set on point, alternated with four white blocks which contain vases of flowers in both corded and stuffed work. The eight half blocks and four corner triangles were filled with the same design elements, adapted to fit the space. The background quilting was done in parallel lines approximately ⅓" apart.

Nine large rosettes, with four small rose wreaths between them, grace the surface of a beautiful appliqué quilt documented by the Kansas Quilt Project (Plate 1-18). Nancy Hornback noted that stuffed work in the background areas includes five Classic urns and three flower-filled vases, plus a scattering of feather, floral, and berry designs. According to family history, the maker used a rose thorn to push the stuffing through the back of her quilt. The background quilting was done in straight lines ¼" apart.

Large rose trees and smaller rosettes are framed with a running floral border on this exceptional quilt also documented in Kansas (Plate 1-19). Corded and stuffed motifs include a pair of Classic urns filled with a lavish display of floral and pineapple motifs, plus six narrow panels of berry-laden vines. The background quilting was done in approximately ½" grid and is exceptionally fine with between 14 and 19 stitches to the inch.

Unusual in several ways, the all-white quilt from the Smithsonian collection in Plate 1-27 on page 18, contains designs which would have been more typically found on mid-century appliqué album quilts. Worked one block at a time, the motifs were machine outline quilted, and then stuffed. Only the quilting which frames each block was done by hand. There is no background quilting.

Cording and stuffing were sometimes used to create dimension within appliqué pieces such as the elaborate work found on Baltimore album quilts and other appliqué quilts of the mid-nineteenth century. Two beautiful red and green quilts from the collection of Sara Dillow of Fremont, Nebraska, include appliquéd and stuffed flowers. In the first quilt (Plate 1-20), stuffing has been used to fill quilted sections within star-shaped flowers which are set in a traditional wreath pattern. In an unusual rose medallion quilt (Plate 1-21), stuffing has been added behind the roses and also behind the yellow circles which form a swag border around the quilt.

Although, in most parts of the country, the Civil War seems to have brought an end to such time-intensive quiltmaking, the tradition of raised work continued in some areas. Bets Ramsey and Merikay Waldvogel found that quiltmakers in Rhea County, Tennessee, continued to add stuffed work to their quilts until just after the turn of the century. The Irish Chain quilt in Plate 1-22, on page 17, is typical of these quilts in which the designs were generally larger in scale and less refined, but worked in the same manner.

Some early quiltmakers also added stuffing through an inner layer which was basted behind the top before it was layered for quilting. When studying antique quilts with stuffed work, an inner layer may be visible if the quilt is held up to the light or placed on a light box.

Several twentieth century quiltmakers found this interlining technique to be useful. In 1933 Margaret Caden's quilt, "Star of the Bluegrass," was the winner of the Century of Progress contest sponsored by Sears, Roebuck and Company. The quilt was composed of 42 Eight-pointed Stars, with stuffed fern or feather motifs in the sashing and borders. It is reported that the stuffed work elicited great praise from the judges and viewers at the exposition. According to Merikay Waldvogel and Barbara Brackman, work on the quilt had actually been hired out to several quiltmakers, rather than being done by Miss Caden. Surviving sample blocks made by Mattie Clark Black of Lexington, Kentucky, show how the stuffing was added through an inner

△ **Plate 1-19.** "Rose Tree," made by Sarah Jane Work Denny, 85" x 93", Pennsylvania, 1845–65. Collection of Hazel Craig. Photo courtesy of Nancy Hornback.

△ **Plate 1-20.** Detail of Rose Wreath with stuffed appliqué flowers. Collection of Sara Rhodes Dillow, Fremont, Nebraska.

△ **Plate 1-21.** Detail of Medallion Floral Wreath with stuffed appliqué. Collection of Sara Rhodes Dillow.

△ **Plate 1-22.** *"Double Irish Chain," made by Eleanor Wilson Broyles, Rhea Co., TN, 1886. Collection of Bettye J. Broyles. Photo courtesy of* Quilts of Tennessee, *Bets Ramsey and Merikay Waldvogel.*

layer stitched behind the quilt top (Plate 1-23).

Surface quilting within a raised work design is another indication that some of the work was done before the quilt was layered for final quilting. Award-winning quiltmaker Bertha Stenge of Illinois, also used the interlining technique when she made her beautiful "Tiger Lily" quilt about 1940 (Plate 1-24). A look at the raised work from the front and from the back reveals that the quilting within the motif is worked through the two layers of the top and the interlining (Plates 1-25 and 1-26). Only

△ **Plate 1-25.** *Detail from "Tiger Lily," quilt showing surface quilting.*

△ **Plate 1-23.** *Sample block made by Mattie Clark Black, 1933. Photo courtesy of Merikay Waldvogel, Knoxville, Tennessee.*

△ **Plate 1-24.** *A block from "Tiger Lily," Made by Bertha Sheram Stenge, c. 1940. Collection of Joyce Gross, Petaluma, California.*

△ **Plate 1-26.** *Detail from "Tiger Lily," showing only outline quilting on back.*

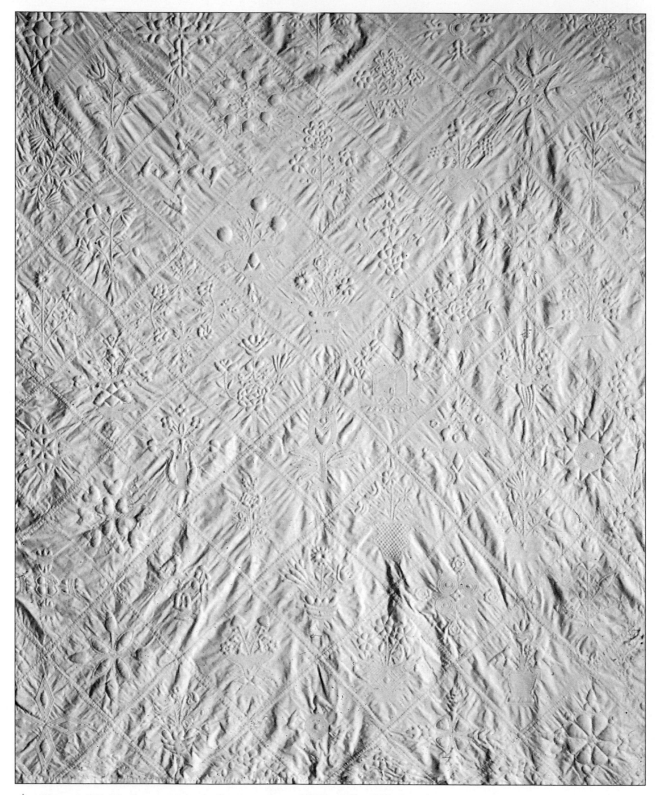

△ *Plate 1-27. Machine stitched album quilt, c. 1860, 76" x 63". Smithsonian collection.*

△ **Plate 1-28.** *Brochure of quilt pattern "intended as a special service to users of Mountain Mist Quilt Fillings — to provide them with designs that are better than ordinary and at a modest price." Author's collection.*

the outline of the motif is quilted through to the back. The Tiger Lily block also shows a unique combination of appliqué and raised work in which the two techniques have been used to create an intermeshed design. Corded work alone forms the border wreath patterns. The background quilting is worked in crosshatch with a very fine stitch.

When Anne Orr wrote an article. "Appliqué and Trapunto," in a 1943 *Better Homes & Gardens'* column entitled "Quilt Today," she suggested basting a stamped or marked muslin to the underside of the quilt top in order to add cording or stuffing between the two layers.

Even as late as the 1950's, Mountain Mist quilting patterns included a design called Hanging Gardens (Plate 1-28), described as "an exquisite example of Trapunto or Padded Quilting." The design was copied from a nineteenth century whole cloth quilt and featured a flower-filled cornucopia surrounded by a feather swag border.

With several award-winning quiltmakers featuring stuffed work and leading designers offering instructions, it is curious to note how few twentieth century quiltmakers chose to add this technique to their quilts. For quilts so recently made and of the type which seemingly should have been kept as heirlooms, few with raised work are found today.

△ **Plate 1-29.** *"Tiger Lily," 63" x 79" made by Bertha Sheram Stenge, c. 1940. Collection of Joyce Gross.*

CHAPTER 2

THE
PROCESS

▷ *Plate 2-1. A beautiful example of a quilt worked in colored silk is this exquisite Provencal vanho or small bedcover. The top of the quilt is a warm plum color, and the backing fabric is a rich gold. The piece is quilted in interlocking circles in the center and bordered with running vine and flowers. Vanho, Provence, c. 1870, 58" x 68". Collection of Kathryn Berenson.*

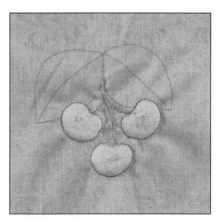

△ *Plate 2-2. Stuffed cherries, wrong side.*

△ *Plate 2-3. Texture of cherries is lost on busy print.*

△ *Plate 2-4. Texture of grapes is lost on mottled fabric.*

MATERIALS

FABRICS

As with any other type of quiltmaking, natural fabrics are probably the best choices for quilts with raised work. 100% cotton seems best for developing texture around stipple quilted areas. Early European quilts of this style were made of cotton, wool, or silk, in white or brilliant solid colors (Plate 2-1).

COLOR CHOICES

Traditional American quilts were most often made of white or natural color cotton. When choosing fabric, keep in mind that the visual effect of this raised work is created by light and shadow and that this texture will be lost on a busy background (Plates 2-2, 2-3, and 2-4).

Good choices include muslin, most solid colors, and sometimes a fine print that reads as a solid. A very traditional look can be achieved by using white or off-white for a whole cloth quilt with raised work. In order to show as much variety as possible, the samples throughout this book were created using a range of light to dark values. Compare the three samples here (Plates 2-5, 2-6, and 2-7), which were worked on light pink, medium purple, and a dark charcoal. Before starting a large project, it would probably be beneficial to make test samples in several values and colors to see which one pleases your eye. Keep in mind that you are looking for a fabric which will show the best contrast of light and shadow created by the raised work and by the texture of the quilted background.

FILLING

INTERLINING

Batiste or some other lightweight fabric will be needed for an inner layer when adding cording or stuffing in whole cloth quilts or in the background areas of patchwork or appliqué quilts (Plate 2-8, page 23). Choose a fabric that is thin, or one with an open weave for ease in inserting the cording or stuffing. Keep in mind that some of this fabric will remain inside the finished quilt and will add an extra layer to be quilted through.

If you are using white or a very light fabric for your quilt top, check to see if the interlining will create a shadow at the edge. You may want to consider leaving a full interlining behind the entire top.

YARN

A synthetic yarn, such as polyester or acrylic, is most commonly used today for corded channel work. Synthetic yarns are compressible and easy to pull through the weave of the fabric; they are also resilient enough to fill the channel completely once they are in place. There is no need to worry about shrinkage with synthetics.

Among the synthetic yarns which work well are acrylic craft or rug yarn, a finer, baby or sport weight knitting yarn, and the larger polyester yarn sold for trapunto work. Although soft polyester yarn works well for filling small spaces, it is sometimes too fragile to be pulled through long channels.

If you prefer to work with cotton, look for a 4-ply cotton crochet or knitting yarn, such as Lily Sugar and Cream™. This yarn is soft, yet sturdy enough to pull through long channels. Most of these yarns can be easily separated into single or double plies for pulling through narrower spaces.

NEEDLES

In choosing needles for corded work, look for a tapestry needle

△ *Plate 2-5. Light pink rosebud.*

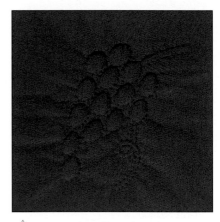

△ *Plate 2-6. Purple grapes.*

△ *Plate 2-7. Charcoal teardrop flower.*

△ *Plate 2-8. Back of sample block showing batiste as inner layer.*

in a size 16 or 18. It is important that the needle have a blunt end so that it will slide easily through the channel and not get caught in the fabric. The needle must also have an eye large enough to be threaded with a heavy yarn. The length of the needle is not so important; a shorter one is better for filling curved channels.

PADDING

Another method for raising an area up from the surface of the quilt is by padding the design with pieces of batting cut to fit the shape. When choosing a batting for this technique, my preference is one with good loft, and stable enough to maintain its shape when cut. A cotton/polyester blend batt seems to be the best choice. Fairfield Cotton Classic provides a dense, solid padding for a nineteenth century feel. Use one or two layers for the amount of loft desired. Hobbs Heirloom® Cotton blend is lighter weight, more stable, and higher in loft. One layer of this batting will produce a beautifully raised, slightly softer effect. Both of these battings will cut a clean shape and are stable enough to stay in place without being quilted through.

STUFFING

When adding stuffing to a motif, I usually prefer the solid, traditional feel of cotton. Cotton fiber has several other advantages. It will cling to a small stuffing tool or a wooden toothpick for easy insertion and it is opaque, for a cleaner, whiter appearance in raised areas. Cotton fibers will sometimes cause an uneven fill or a lumpy surface. If you find this is the case, the area might need more stuffing to fill it out completely, or it might need rearranging for a more even fill. Be careful that you do not fill the space so tightly as to cause distortion of the surrounding areas.

Polyester fibers can also be used for stuffing. Polyester lends a softer effect, for a more contemporary look. You may find that the soft polyester fibers fill the space more evenly, with perhaps less distortion of surrounding areas. Because polyester is translucent, it may produce a slightly gray appearance in white or light colors, but will not cause a problem behind darker colored fabrics. Bearding may be more likely with loose polyester fibers and will be distracting on a dark surface. Polyester fibers are slippery and springy, making them more difficult to push into place.

A cotton/polyester blend may offer the best of both fibers for stuffed work. Blends have a softer texture and more loft than cotton, but feel more solid than polyester.

When adding stuffing to a motif, take care to see that the filling is evenly distributed and that it fills the space completely (Plate 2-9). A space which is only partially filled will not have the same impact as one which stands up fully from the surface. The finished effect in both texture and visual impact should be worth the time and effort spent on creating the work.

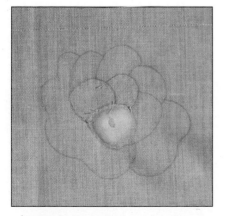

△ *Plate 2-9. Space is not sufficiently filled.*

BASTING

△ *Plate 2-10. Motif basted behind block.*

△ *Plate 2-11. Machine basting with water-soluble thread.*

Because all of the raised work is added behind the quilt top, these areas will be basted as a first step and then be quilted through all layers after the quilt top is layered with batting and back. This may seem like extra work, but you will find that the basting goes quickly and the finished effect, with no damage to the quilt lining, is worth the extra effort.

There are several ways to approach the first step of adding cording, padding, or stuffing to the quilt top.

1. Baste the interlining or the padding behind the quilt top, just inside the marked quilting line, in areas which will have raised work (Plate 2-10). After the raised work is done and the quilt has been layered, quilt on the marked line to hold the cording, padding, or stuffing in place. The basting stitches are temporary, but should not be large. They must be fine enough to hold the filling in place. You may want to stitch with contrasting thread which will be more easily seen for removal, but be aware that dark threads may leave a trace of their color behind. Leave the knot of the basting thread on the right side of the quilt top for easy removal.

2. A water soluble thread, used in Plate 2-11, can save one step in the basting process, as there is no need to remove it. This thread will dissolve when the finished piece is washed. When using this thread, you may baste more closely along the pattern lines, as the quilting can be stitched directly over the first line with no worry about removing the basting thread. Wash-out thread is also a good choice for machine work, either twin needle for channels or free-motion basting for stuffed or padded work, because the bobbin thread will also disappear when the piece is washed. This thread is fairly strong and stands up to the strain of pulling cording through a channel or stuffing a space, but may break down in humid conditions or over a long period of time.

3. Some complex patterns will have the outside edges basted and the interior lines quilted through the top and interlining (Plate 2-12). The interior quilting is finished in this first step. Only the outline will be quilted through all layers, after the quilt has been layered with the batting and back.

4. Designs with adjacent raised areas may be simpler to stitch if the lines dividing these areas are quilted first with a fine thread and again with quilting thread through all layers (Plate 2-13). This technique is best used if your quilting stitches are very small and will not show as two lines of stitching.

△ *Plate 2-12. Rose and buds with interior lines quilted to batiste.*

△ *Plate 2-13. Feather with center vein line re-quilted.*

DESIGNS

Designs for whole cloth work can be in any style. Don't shy away from complex designs. One of the real freedoms of raised work is that there are no edges to turn. Sharp points and intricate shapes can be created with raised work much more easily than perhaps is possible with appliqué.

Designs chosen for raised work used in combination with patchwork or appliqué blocks should complement those other elements in size, style, mood, and balance. Plate 2-14 shows a pieced cherry basket with corded and padded cherries added as raised work designs. The appliquéd and embroidered evergreen wreath in Plate 2-15 is complemented by corded snowflakes.

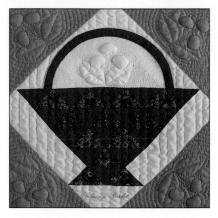

△ *Plate 2-14. Cherry basket with corded and padded cherries.*

△ *Plate 2-15. Corded snow-flakes complement evergreen wreath.*

APPROACHES TO THE WORK

CUTTING BACKGROUND BLOCKS

Both raised work and fine background quilting can shrink an area greatly and distort the lines of a quilt. Plate 2-16 shows how a heavily stuffed motif and stipple quilted background, done after the quilt was pieced, have caused distortion of the seam line.

There is great advantage in working a quilt block by block, or in sections, even when the finished piece will have a whole cloth look. You will find that there will be much less distortion if the raised work patterns are done individually and the blocks are trimmed to final size before they are set together. The piece can then be layered with batting and the back, and quilted as a whole.

MARKING THE PATTERN ON THE QUILT TOP

The most basic approach for marking a design for raised work is the same as for marking any other quilting pattern. Position the design, right side up, under the quilt top or block, and trace it onto the fabric. It is perhaps easier to get an exact placement of the pattern when working from the right side. Marking on the front also provides the most accurate pattern for quilting. Use light or removable marks that will not be distracting in the finished piece. Because these blocks will be pressed and trimmed to size before they are set together for quilting, it is important that the marker which you use is heat safe.

△ *Plate 2-16. Stuffed work and stipple quilting may distort seam lines.*

If the design is to be corded, position a layer of batiste, cut slightly larger than the pattern, behind the block and pin or baste the edges in place. Baste just inside the marked quilting lines to hold the two layers of fabric together. Cord the design, using a tapestry needle and yarn to fill each of the spaces between the quilt block and the interlining (Plate 2-17).

For stuffed work, mark the design on the top of the block and add a layer of batiste behind. Use a basting stitch just inside the marked quilting lines to define the pattern and hold the two layers of fabric together. Turn the piece to the wrong side and add stuffing by working through small holes made in the interlining (Plate 2-18).

For padded work, no interlining is needed. Simply position a piece of batting behind the motif and baste from the front, just inside the drawn lines. Turn the piece to the wrong side and trim the batting close to the basting line (Plate 2-19). Small scissors with sharp, narrow blades will be very helpful for close trimming. Another option for padded work is to add a layer or two of padding, pre-cut to shape, to fill a specific motif.

WORKING FROM BEHIND

Occasionally you may find that you are using a fabric that you cannot or do not want to mark on the front. Working from behind will be helpful for dark fabrics which may be difficult to see through, fabrics that you may not want to mark, such as silk, or fabric which might be difficult to mark, such as velvet. There are several options for working from the wrong side of the fabric.

MARKING ON THE INTERLINING

Marking the pattern on the interlining is one way to transfer the design without marks on the quilt top (Plate 2-20, page 27). Remember that the pattern must be reversed when it is traced onto the batiste. You may also find that more care is required in positioning the pattern from the wrong side. Once the interlining is in place, baste just inside the marked lines and cord or stuff the design, as before.

MARKING ON THE BACK

Marking the pattern directly onto the back of the quilt top works best for padded work (Plate 2-21, page 27). The padded pieces, cut to shape, can be set into place within the marked lines and basted into place from behind. Remember that an asymmetrical pattern will need to be reversed when it is marked from the wrong side. Keep in mind that marks may show through a very sheer fabric, even when it is marked on the wrong side.

NO MARKS

It is possible to prepare a design with no marks at all, for a completely clean surface. If the quilt top is muslin or a light color, position the pattern and the quilt top *Both* wrong side up on a light box.

△ **Plate 2-17.** *Basted and corded channels.*

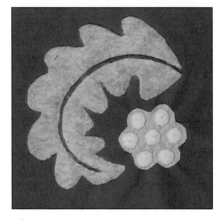

△ **Plate 2-18.** *Motif basted and stuffed through batiste layer.*

△ **Plate 2-19.** *Padded motif basted into place.*

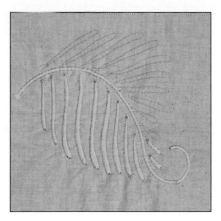

△ *Plate 2-20. Design marked on batiste.*

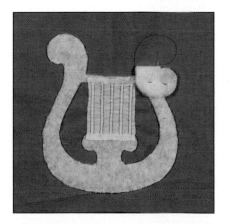

△ *Plate 2-21. Design marked on back of block.*

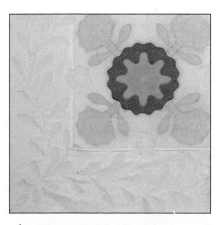

△ *Plate 2-22. Padding and cording placed with no marks.*

Padding pieces pre-cut to shape may be positioned and pinned to the wrong side of the quilt top without any markings. Baste around the edges to hold the padding in place until the quilt is layered with the batting and back (Plate 2-22).

All of these approaches, with no marks on the top, require that the quilting be done by eye or by feel. Careful basting around the edges will help to preserve the outline. Often the padding will produce a slight value change, making the edge easy to identify. Or, you may feel the edge of the padding when quilting around it. This works well for leaves or simple shapes. If you are working with intricately shaped motifs, you may need to think about how to maintain that shape when quilting. A freezer paper or Contac™ paper shape positioned on top of the padded area can give you an exact outline to follow when quilting, if necessary.

EMBROIDERY OUTLINE

Any motif may be defined and enhanced with embroidery before it is padded or stuffed (Plate 2-23). Mark the design on the quilt top; the lines will be covered by the embroidery stitches. Embroider the line with any thread and the stitch of your choice. You may work a decorative thread through the fabric or couch it by hand or machine.

For corded or stuffed work, cut a piece of interlining fabric slightly larger than the motif and pin or baste the edges in place behind the quilt top. Work the line of embroidery stitches through both the top and the batiste layers. Turn the piece to the wrong side and add cording or stuffing through the interlining (Plate 2-24).

△ *Plate 2-23. Design embroidered with #8 perle cotton and stem stitch, corded and stuffed from behind.*

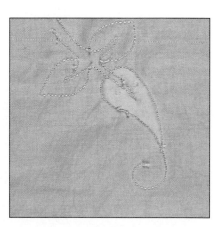

△ *Plate 2-24. Embroidery line holds layers together for stuffed work.*

For padded work, no interlining is needed. Work the line of embroidery stitches through the quilt top only. The padding may be added in either of the ways previously discussed. A layer of padding may be placed behind the motif, basted from the front, just inside the embroidery line and trimmed to fit. The embroidery stitches also provide a good pattern on the reverse side for placement of padding pieces pre-cut to shape, which can then be basted into place from the wrong side (Plate 2-25).

△ *Plate 2-25.* *Pre-cut shapes basted into place within embroidered design.*

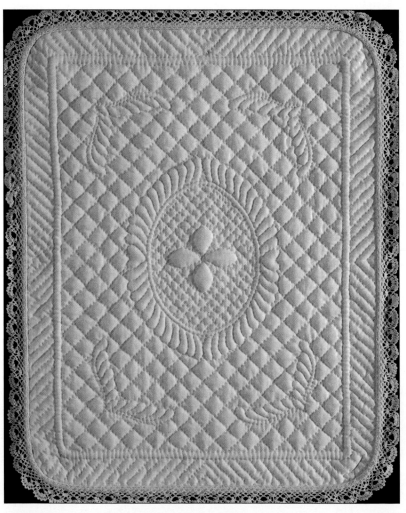

△ *Plate 2-26.* *"Miniature Feathers and Lace," 11" x 13¾", 1992, made by Beverly Mannisto Williams, Cadillac, Michigan. Author's collection. This miniature all white quilt with corded channels and feather designs is finished with a narrow edging of bobbin lace.*

CHAPTER 3

TECHNIQUE SAMPLER

The technique section provides patterns and step-by-step instructions for 25 different approaches to raised work. The small blocks are to be made as practice pieces and may be kept as notebook samples, for reference, as you add raised work to future quilts. They can also be used as joiner blocks for the larger patterns provided, or as blocks in a miniature quilt. The patterns are meant to finish as 3½" blocks. It is a good idea to cut the blocks at least an inch larger and then trim them to size after the raised work is finished.

◁ **Plate 3-1.** *Daisy design with corded flower petals, stems, and leaves.*

CORDED CHANNELS

Cording seems best used for linear designs, such as leaf veins, stem work, narrow petals, grids, basket weave, outlines, letters, or numbers (Plates 3-1 and 3-2).

Below are several suggestions about various types or weights of yarn to fill different sizes of channels.

•For ⅛" wide channel, use 1 strand of craft or rug yarn, 2 strands of sport yarn, or 1 strand of Lily Sugar and Cream™ cotton.

•For ³⁄₁₆" wide channel, use 2 strands of craft or rug yarn, 2 strands of Lily cotton, or 1 ply of a 3-ply polyester trapunto yarn.

•For ¼" wide channel, use 2 plies of polyester trapunto yarn.

◁ **Plate 3-2.** *Example of cording used for letters. Photo courtesy of Kathryn Berenson.*

ANITA SHACKELFORD: SURFACE TEXTURES

▷ *Plate 3-3. Flower with corded stem.*

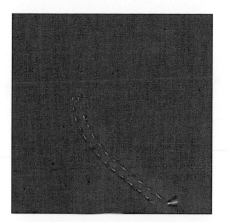

△ *Plate 3-3a. Basted and corded channel, right side.*

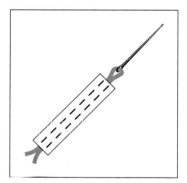

△ *Fig. 1. Tapestry needle and yarn are used to cord channel.*

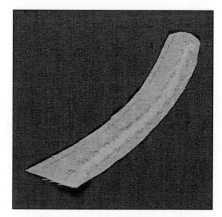

△ *Plate 3-3b. Basted and corded channel, wrong side. One side trimmed.*

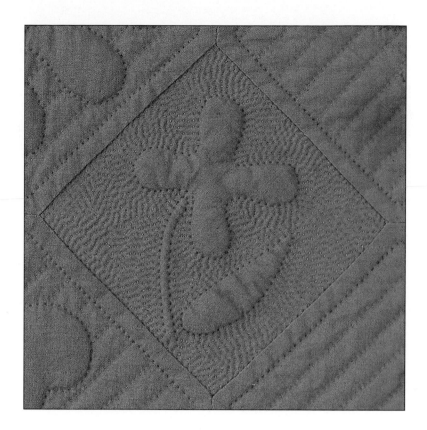

PROJECT #1: FLOWER STEM — CORDED CHANNEL

A basic stem is marked on the front of the block, and has a bias strip of batiste positioned on the back. Basting stitches along both sides create a channel to hold the cording in place until the piece is layered for quilting. Cut the strip of batiste three times the finished width of the channel. The excess will be trimmed away after the cording is in place. The extra width of the bias strip allows for some flexibility in placement, especially on curved stems.

Pin the strip of batiste in place behind the marked stem, and baste just inside the channel lines. Leave the beginning knot on the right side of the block and end the basting line with a backstitch (Plate 3-3a).

Thread a tapestry needle with a single yarn or pull the yarn through the eye for a double strand. To add the cording, enter under the batiste at one end of the channel and slide the needle between the layers (Fig. 1).

Work the needle along the channel and pull the yarn through to fill the entire length. It is an easy matter to slide the needle in and out with both ends of the channel open. Check the right side of the fabric to make sure that the yarn has not penetrated the top. Pull to smooth out the channel, but take care not to overstretch the bias of the fabric. Trim off the yarn tails at each end of the stem. Trim away the excess batiste along both sides of the channel, leaving approximately ⅛" on all sides (Plate 3-3b).

◁ **Plate 3-4.** *Complex corded motif will require full interlining.*

△ **Plate 3-4a.** *Daisy motif basted and corded, right side.*

When designing or adapting designs with stems, you may choose to end the stem within the block. If the stem extends to the edge of the block, it is better to finish at a seam on one side rather than in a corner where there are many seam allowances.

If you are using a double strand, separate the yarns before beginning, otherwise they may twist and create an uneven surface texture in the channel, with something of a "barber pole" effect. This problem seems to be much more noticeable with cotton yarn.

With some very narrow stems, basting inside the lines may make the channel too narrow for the needle to pass. Working with a smaller needle, such as a size 20 may help. You might also consider basting directly on the line and removing the basting stitches just ahead of the quilting stitches, or basting with wash-out thread and quilting directly over the basting stitches.

PROJECT #2: DAISY — CORDED WITH FULL INTERLINING

When more complex designs are to be filled with cording, it is more efficient to work with a square of batiste behind the full design space. The stitching and cording progress in a similar manner. Baste each section of the design, just inside the marked lines, to create the channels for cording (Plate 3-4a). When adding cording through this full interlining, you may find that you will need to make a small opening in order to begin a line. Pick up the layer of batiste with a

△ **Plate 3-4b.** *Daisy block basted and corded, wrong side.*

▷ *Plate 3-5.* Corded rings.

△ *Plate 3-5a.* *Basted and corded rings, right side.*

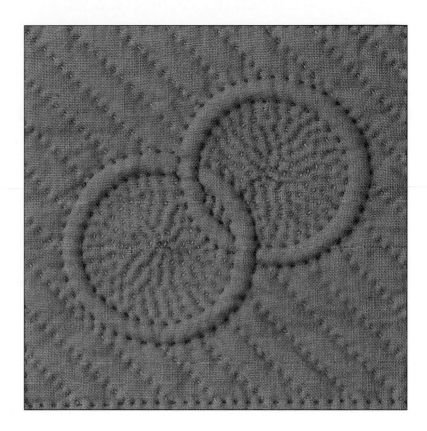

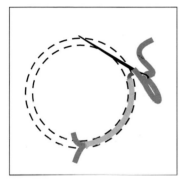

△ *Fig. 2.* *Repositioning needle in curved channel.*

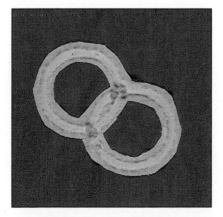

△ *Plate 3-5b.* *Basted and corded rings, wrong side.*

toothpick or a seam ripper, if your blunt needle will not penetrate the fabric. Take care to make the hole in the batiste layer only! Fill each channel individually, trimming the yarn ends close to the fabric. When the cording is finished, trim the batiste, leaving approximately ⅛" around the design (Plate 3-4b, page 32).

When cording tapered channels, work from the large end to the small end, taking the needle as far as it will reasonably go. You may also find it helpful to leave a ⅛" to ¼" tail to be stuffed in to fill the larger end.

If a larger channel requires pulling yarn through a second time, for a total of 3 or 4 yarns, enter through a separate hole to avoid catching the tails and disturbing the placement of the first strands. Wait to trim all of the tails until after you are satisfied that the channel is sufficiently filled.

PROJECT #3: RINGS — CORDED CURVES

Curves and circles require the use of a full piece of batiste behind them and also present unique problems in pulling the cording through.

Curved designs can be marked on the front and basted just inside the marked lines (Plate 3-5a). To cord a curve, begin by going through the batiste layer and working the needle and yarn as far as possible. When it is necessary to reposition the needle, come out through the batiste layer or between the basting stitches, insert the needle back into the same hole and again, travel as far as possible (Fig. 2).

◁ **Plate 3-6.** *Corded channel with sharp point.*

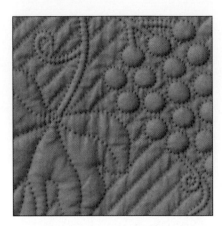

△ **Plate 3-5c.** *Corded tendrils.*

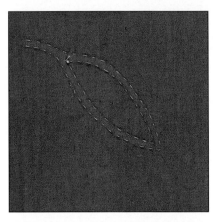

△ **Plate 3-6a.** *Pointed shape basted and corded, right side.*

A tight curve may need to be corded in three or four sections. Pull carefully so that the yarn does not draw up the channel. Smooth the fabric completely each time, before doing the next section. If you find that there is too much distortion, remember that you can always remove the cord and try again. Trim the ends of the cord after you are certain that it is right. Trim the batiste layer both inside and outside the circles (Plate 3-5b, page 33).

When only part of a channel is curved, such as a grape tendril, cord the straight area first. Smooth the yarn and fabric into place and then cord the curve, a small amount at a time (Fig. 3-5c)

PROJECT #4: TEAR DROP FLOWER — CORDED POINT

Corded channels with sharp points present another problem. If pulled too tightly, the cord will pull too far back into the channel and cause the pointed end to be rounded instead. To prevent this from happening, leave a small stitch of yarn outside of the interlining to keep the yarn in its correct position.

For this project, mark the design on the right side of block (Plate 3-6a), position a layer of batiste behind, and baste and cord the channels as shown in Plate 3-6b. Refer to stuffed work project #16 to finish the tear drop petals on this flower.

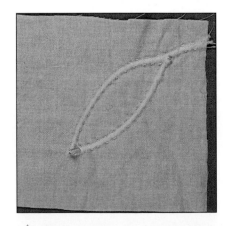

△ **Plate 3-6b.** *Pointed shape basted and corded, wrong side, showing small stitch of yarn left outside of batiste.*

▷ *Plate 3-7.* Cherries on branching stems.

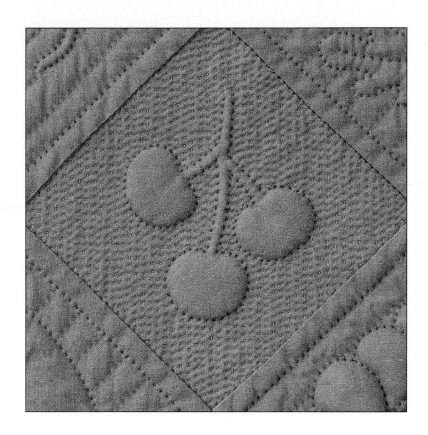

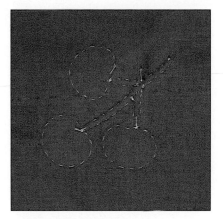

△ *Plate 3-7a.* Basted and corded stems, right side.

PROJECT #5: CHERRIES — BRANCHING STEMS

Branching stems can be done with separate strips of batiste or with a full layer behind the motif, depending on the complexity of the design. Begin by basting inside the channel lines, as before (Plate 3-7a). Cord the main stem first. When filling the side stems, pull the cord toward, and actually into, the main stem channel so that the tail is anchored and will not slip out of position (Plate 3-7b).

△ *Plate 3-7b.* Basted and corded stems, wrong side, showing full interlining and yarn being pulled through.

◁ *Plate 3-7c.* Finished Cherry Wreath block.

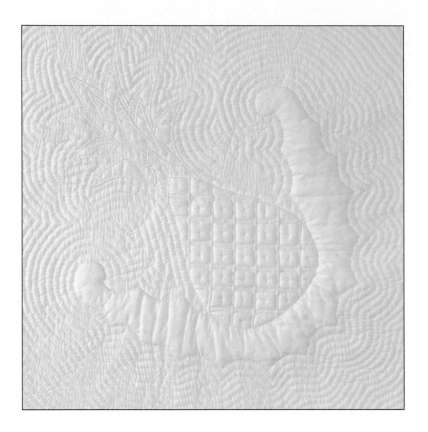

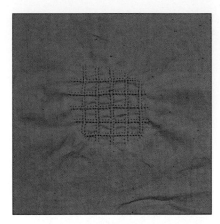

◁ *Plate 3-8. Detail of quilted pineapple with channels which cross.*

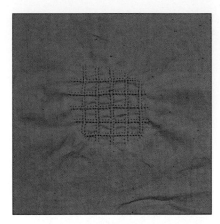

△ *Plate 3-8a. Crossed channels, quilted and corded, right side.*

PROJECT #6: PINEAPPLE — CROSSED CHANNELS

Interior lines which cross each other or appear to be woven, as in a pineapple or basket may be approached in two different ways.

Position a full interlining behind the area to be corded. If the small squares between the corded channels are to be left flat, the lines will be basted and corded, as before, with final quilting through all layers.

For a motif, such as this pineapple, with sections which will be stuffed, use quilting thread and a fine quilting stitch to quilt the block and the interlining together along each channel line (Plate 3-8a). These lines will not be re-quilted. It is probably easiest to cord all channels in one direction before beginning the channels in the other direction. A size 20 needle will be helpful for cording a small channel and for pulling the second set of yarn through the first. If you have difficulty in pulling one through the other, pass the needle over or under the first cord, remaining inside the channel.

Leave small tails of yarn at the beginning and at the end of each channel until all are finished. This is especially important when yarns cross through one another and may pull and shorten each other. Trim the yarn tails when all of the corded and stuffed work is finished (Plate 3-8b). See technique #19 for instructions on finishing the pineapple sections which are to be stuffed and tacked.

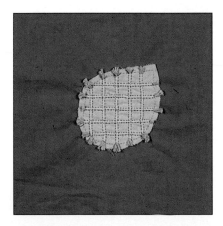

△ *Plate 3-8b. Crossed channels, wrong side, showing strands of yarn pulled through one another.*

▷ *Plate 3-9.* *Block with padded flower and leaf.*

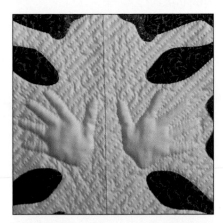

△ *Plate 3-9a.* *Silhouette of baby's hands done with padded technique.*

△ *Plate 3-9b.* *Basted and padded flower and leaf, right side.*

△ *Plate 3-9c.* *Basted and padded flower and leaf, wrong side.*

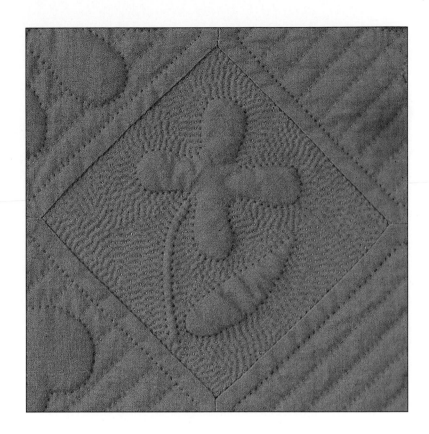

PADDED WORK

Padding creates a smoother, flatter finish in raised work. It is a good choice for intricate designs such as leaves, scrollwork, solid lettering, and silhouettes, such as faces, hands (Plate 3-9a), birds, and other animals.

PROJECT #7: FOUR PETAL FLOWER — PADDED, MARKED ON THE FRONT

For simple flowers and leaves, a layer of padding will create a beautiful raised effect. Go back to the little block from project #1 to add the padded flower and leaf. Position a small piece of batting behind the flower shape and secure it with a pin in each petal. Working from the front, baste just inside the marked line to hold the batting in place and to define the outline (Plate 3-9b). Turn the block to the wrong side and trim the batting close to the stitched line, leaving just enough to pad the motif (Plate 3-9c). Repeat the same process for the leaf. Use small sharp scissors for best control and take care when trimming that you do not cut the fabric. Save the batting scraps for the stuffed work to follow.

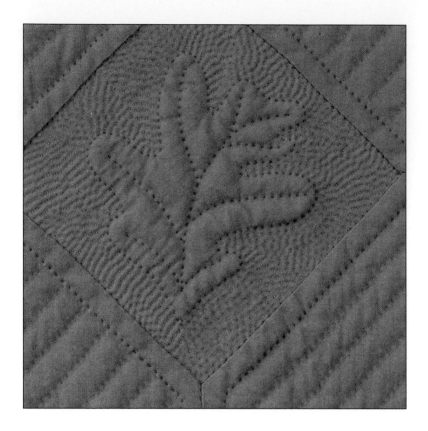

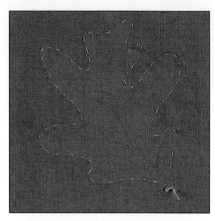

◁ *Plate 3-10.* Padded oak leaf with interior lines quilted through all layers.

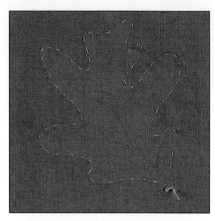

△ *Plate 3-10a.* Basted and padded leaf, right side.

PROJECT #8: OAK LEAF —
PADDED, WITH INTERIOR LINES QUILTED THROUGH ALL LAYERS

Many padded motifs, such as leaves and flowers, have interior lines which help add detail and definition to them. Mark the outline and the interior lines of the design on the front of the block. In this case, the stitching will be done in two separate steps. Baste around the edges, just inside the marked line, and trim to fit, as before (Plates 3-10a and 3-10b). After the quilt has been layered for quilting, the interior lines will be quilted through all layers, including both layers of batting, for deeper definition of the vein lines.

△ *Plate 3-10b.* Basted and padded leaf, wrong side.

◁*Plate 3-10c.* Jacobean design includes padded flower and leaf, detailed by quilting through all layers.

▷ *Plate 3-11.* *Padded leaf with open center channel.*

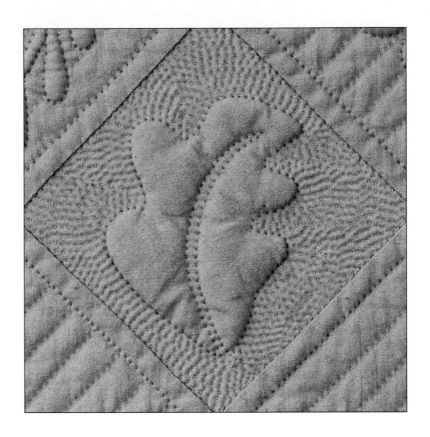

△ *Plate 3-11a. Basted and padded leaf, right side.*

△ *Plate 3-11b. Basted and padded leaf, wrong side, showing batting cut away from center channel.*

PROJECT #9: LEAF — PADDED, WITH OPEN CENTER CHANNEL

If quilting through an extra layer of batting seems too difficult, one solution is to redesign the motif with an open area where the quilted line is desired. This leaf has a double channel line along the center vein which should be basted and trimmed in the same manner as the outside edge (Plates 3-11a and 3-11b). Removing this small line of batting from the center of the leaf will make the quilting much easier and provide somewhat the same definition as the padded leaf with the interior lines quilted through all layers.

◁*Plate 3-11c. Leaf and Berries block includes padded leaf with open center channel.*

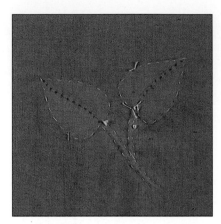

◁ *Plate 3-12. Leaves with surface quilting for vein lines.*

△ *Plate 3-12a. Basted, padded, and corded block, right side, with vein lines quilted through padding.*

PROJECT #10: LITTLE LEAF VEINS — PADDED, WITH SURFACE QUILTING

Surface quilting provides another option to adding detail to a padded motif. These little leaves are to be padded, basted, and trimmed around the outside edges, as in technique #7 (Plate 3-12a). To stitch the center vein, place a strip of batiste behind the vein line and quilt through all three layers (Plate 3-12b). This process produces a quilted texture on a raised motif, without quilting through two layers of batting. Be sure to quilt through all three layers rather than only the two layers of the quilt block and padding. The third layer of fabric is necessary to support the underneath stitches which would otherwise sink too deeply into the batting and create little or no texture on the surface.

△ *Plate 3-12b. Basted, padded, and corded block, wrong side, showing batiste layer to support quilted lines.*

ANITA SHACKELFORD: SURFACE TEXTURES

▷ *Plate 3-13. Leaf with a corded vein.*

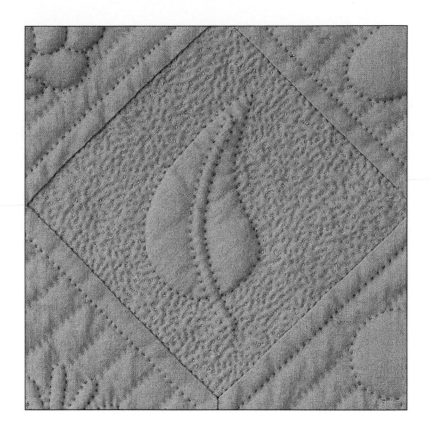

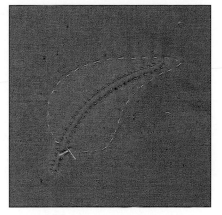

△ *Plate 3-13a. Quilted and corded vein line, right side.*

PROJECT #11: LEAF WITH CORDED VEIN — CORDED AND PADDED

Another option for adding a textured vein line is to quilt and cord a channel before positioning the leaf behind it. Mark the leaf design on the front of the block. Place a strip of batiste behind the vein line and quilt along both sides of the channel, using quilting thread and a fine stitch (Plates 3-13a and 3-13b). Cord the channel as in technique #1 and pad the leaf, using technique #7. When the quilt is layered for final quilting, the vein line will not have to be re-quilted through so many layers.

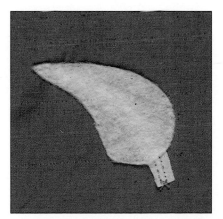

△ *Plate 3-13b. Padded leaf basted in place behind corded vein.*

◁*Plate 3-13c. Finished Rose block includes leaf with corded vein.*

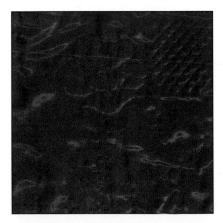

△ *Plate 3-14a.* Detail padded and quilted motif in Yukata fabric.

△ *Plate 3-14b.* Lining of Kimmee coat, showing quilting detail.

PROJECT #12: YUKATA OR SPECIAL FABRIC, PADDED PRINT

Some fabrics offer an opportunity to use raised work for a special effect. When making this kimono jacket, I wanted to emphasize many of the designs in the beautiful Yukata fabrics. The process for padding these motifs is the same as when working with a drawn design; simply place batting behind the motif, baste it in place from the front, and trim to fit the design (Plate 3-14). The final quilting goes through all layers to hold the batting in place and to define the beautiful printed design. Interior design lines may also be quilted, if desired (Plates 3-14a and 3-14b).

Adding padding to fabrics with large scale prints or stylish designs can add beautiful dimension to an otherwise flat surface. For other ideas on using raised work in combination with printed fabrics, refer to page 61 for home decorating and children's quilts.

▷ *Plate 3-15. Corded and padded Laurel Leaf block.*

△ *Plate 3-15a. Basted, padded, and corded block, right side.*

△ *Plate 3-15b. Basted, padded, and corded block, showing placement marks on wrong side.*

PROJECT #13: LAUREL LEAF — MARKED ON THE BACK

Here is a simple design to practice working from the back of the block. Make a paper template and pin it to the batting to cut three leaf shapes for the padded work. Place both the pattern and the block wrong side up on a light box and mark the design on the wrong side of the block. Position the top leaf and baste it into place. Position a strip of batiste for the stem and baste the channel lines. If you find it difficult to see the stem lines, go back to the pattern and mark the channel lines onto the batiste. Add cording and trim the batiste before positioning the leaves along the sides (Plates 3-15a and 3-15b). Remember to leave the knot on the right side when you baste these padded shapes, and take care to baste accurately and close to the edge. With no marks on the right side, the basting stitches will be the guide for your quilting line.

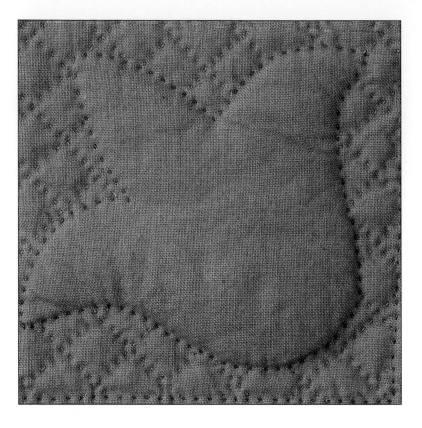

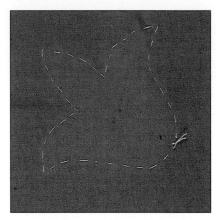

△ **Plate 3-16a.** *Basted, padded tulip, with no marks on right side.*

PROJECT #14: TULIP — NO MARKS

Try this simple tulip shape for practice in positioning a padded motif with no marks at all. Make a paper template for the tulip and cut the shape from a layer of batting. Turn both the pattern and the fabric, wrong side up on a light box for the design placement. Pin the tulip in place and then baste from the wrong side, carefully following the edges to transfer the outline of the shape to the right side of the block (Plates 3-16a and 3-16b). With no marks on the fabric, the basting stitches will be the guide for your outline quilting.

△ **Plate 3-16b.** *Basted, padded tulip, wrong side.*

◁ **Plate 3-16c.** *Finished Tulip block.*

▷ **Plate 3-17.** Flower motif, embroidered and padded.

△ **Plate 3-17a.** Embroidered and padded flower, right side.

△ **Plate 3-17b.** Embroidered flower, wrong side, showing padding set into place.

PROJECT #15: SIX PETAL FLOWER — EMBROIDERED AND PADDED

A motif may be enhanced with embroidery stitches before it is padded. For this sample, a #8 perle cotton and a stem stitch were used to outline the flower motif (Plate 3-17a). Because the embroidery line shows on the wrong side, it is a simple matter to cut batting to shape and set it into place behind the motif (Plate 3-17b). Or, if you prefer, the batting may be basted into place, with stitches just inside the line of embroidery, and then trimmed to fit, as in technique #7. Take care when trimming the padding close to the embroidery, so that you do not inadvertently cut the embroidery thread.

◁ *Plate 3-18. Stuffed sun-flower petals.*

△ *Plate 3-18a. Nineteenth century stuffed work block, 10" x 10½". Gift to the author from Terry Thompson.*

STUFFED WORK

Use stuffed work for small rounded motifs, such as fruit and feathers or small sub-units within a larger motif, such as a pineapple, a sunflower center, rose petals, basket, or vase sections (Plate 3-18a).

Stuffed work is done with an interlining behind the design. This inner layer will allow the stuffing to be added from the wrong side with no worry about causing damage to the back of the quilt.

Use a small pair of scissors or a seam ripper to lift the batiste layer away from the quilt top and make a small hole in the batiste for ease in adding the stuffing. If you make this small cut on the bias, you will find that the opening has more give and will ravel less. Stuff the sections with small pinches of batting saved from the previous padded work. Several tools can be used to insert stuffing into tiny places. Try a small stuffing tool, a wooden toothpick, or a Purple Thang™.

Stuff corners and narrow points first. Try to fill the spaces evenly, using small pinches or narrow wisps of batting. When using a longer strip of batting, start by pushing one end into the opening and the rest will follow easily. *Be careful* not to poke through to the right side of the block. If the opening in the batiste is small, it should not be necessary to stitch it closed.

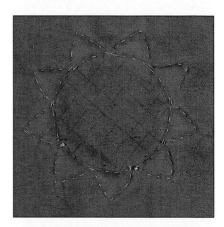

△ *Plate 3-18b. Basted and stuffed flower petals, right side.*

△ *Plate 3-18c. Basted flower petals, wrong side. Stuffing was added through small holes in batiste layer.*

▷ *Plate 3-19. Stuffed-work flower.*

△ *Plate 3-19a. Basted and stuffed flower, showing no marks on right side.*

△ *Plate 3-19b. Basted and stuffed flower, motif marked on batiste.*

PROJECT #16: SUNFLOWER — STUFFED, MARKED ON THE FRONT

Stitch this sunflower for a sample of stuffed work, marked on the front of the block (Plate 3-18b, page 46). Place a square of batiste behind the sunflower design and baste just inside each petal (Plate 3-18b, page 46). Cut a small hole in the batiste behind each petal and stuff each one with small wisps of cotton. Make sure that the petals are stuffed equally and that the corners are filled completely. When the stuffed work is finished, trim away the extra batiste both inside and outside the ring of petals (Plate 3-18c, page 46).

PROJECT #17: EIGHT PETAL FLOWER — STUFFED, MARKED ON THE INTERLINING

For a clean surface, a design for stuffed work can also be marked on the interlining and worked from the back. This eight petal flower design is symmetrical and so can be traced directly onto the batiste. If the design is asymmetrical, turn the pattern over to trace a reverse image. Center the design carefully on the back of the block and pin to hold it in place. Be sure to baste inside the lines to leave room for quilting between the petals. Cut a small hole in the batiste behind each petal and stuff each one with small wisps of cotton (Plates 3-19a and 3-19b). As with the padded work which was marked on the back, this design will be quilted from the right side with only the basting stitches as a guide.

◁ *Plate 3-20.* *Quilted rosebud block, stuffed in units.*

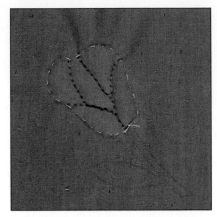

△ *Plate 3-20a.* *Rosebud with outline basted and interior lines quilted, right side.*

Interior lines in some motifs are best quilted to the batiste and not re-quilted. Once these interior lines are quilted, they are finished. The outside lines of these shapes are basted to the batiste, as shown in the rose bud, and will be quilted after the quilt top is layered with batting and back.

PROJECT #18: ROSE BUD — STUFFED IN UNITS

Begin a motif to be stuffed in units by basting around the outside edge. Interior lines, which are to be quilted to the batiste, will then be easier to identify. Use a fine quilting stitch to quilt the block to the batiste. Stuff each section through a small hole in the batiste layer, again making sure to fill them evenly and completely (Plates 3-20a and 3-20b). When the quilt is layered for final quilting, the interior lines will not be re-quilted. Only the outline which is quilted through all layers will show on the back of the quilt.

△ *Plate 3-20b.* *Rosebud, wrong side, showing interior lines quilted to batiste and sections stuffed.*

▷ *Plate 3-21.* Peony motif, stuffed in units.

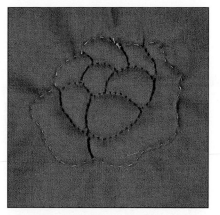

△ *Plate 3-21a.* Peony block, right side with outline basted, interior lines quilted.

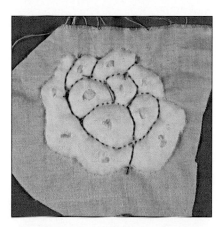

△ *Plate 3-21b.* Peony block, wrong side, showing sections quilted to batiste and stuffed.

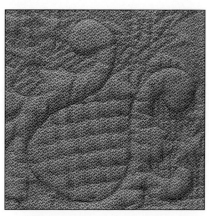

△ *Plate 3-21c.* Detail, back of quilt, showing tacking stitch to secure all layers.

PROJECT #19: PEONY —
STUFFED AND TACKED THROUGH ALL LAYERS

Larger motifs which are surface quilted and not re-quilted will require tacking stitches to hold the backing in place. Begin by basting the outside edges and quilting the interior lines to a layer of batiste, as with the rose bud on page 48. Stuff each section through holes in the interlining. A larger motif may require several openings in some sections for ease in stuffing (Plates 3-21a and 3-21b). When the piece is layered for final quilting, quilt the outline of the flower through all layers. Add tacking stitches, hidden between the stuffed petals to secure the layers behind the flower as shown in the pineapple in Plate 3-21c.

The tacking stitch, worked with quilting thread, comes up through the top, down through all layers, up through the top again, then travels to the next area to be tacked (Fig. 3).

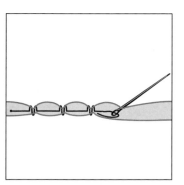

△ *Fig. 3.* Tacking stitch.

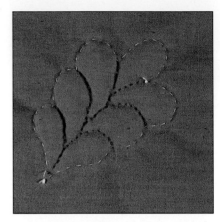

◁ **Plate 3-22.** *Quilted and stuffed feather.*

△ **Plate 3-22a.** *Feather motif, right side, with outline basted and interior lines quilted.*

Although stuffed feathers may be one of the most traditional motifs for stuffed work, they present a technical challenge when the work is done from the inside. As with the peony, heavily stuffed feathers present the problem of quilting between units which are raised. There are several solutions or options to accomplishing beautiful stuffed feather designs.

PROJECT #20: FEATHERS — INTERIOR LINES QUILTED TO INTERLINING

The lines of stitching which divide adjacent raised areas pose a unique problem. Because it is difficult to quilt lines between filled spaces, the final quilting stitch may not be as small as you would like. Feather units can be approached in the same way as the peony, but in most cases tacking through will not provide enough definition in a large feather vein. Quilting once through the top layers and re-quilting the center vein line through all layers may produce a better effect. Begin with a layer of batiste behind the motif, baste along the outside edges and quilt the interior lines (Plates 3-22a and 3-22b). After the quilt is layered with batting and back and the outside edges are quilted, you will see that the center line of the feather may need to be pulled down into place and secured more effectively. Because of the difficulty in quilting between heavily

△ **Plate 3-22b.** *Feather motif, wrong side, showing sections quilted and stuffed.*

▷ *Plate 3-23.* *Quilted feather with open center channel.*

△ *Plate 3-23a.* *Feather motif, right side, with outline and center channel basted.*

△ *Plate 3-23b.* *Feather motif, wrong side, showing sections quilted and stuffed.*

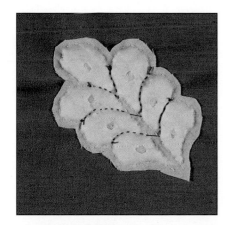

stuffed units, you may find that the stitches in the second line of quilting will be further apart than normal, but this variation will not show as much when worked over a previous line of quilting. You may also want to try quilting this line with a stab stitch, or without a hoop or frame for more flexibility.

PROJECT #21: FEATHER WITH OPEN CENTER

As with the padded leaf in technique #9, you might design a double feather motif with an open channel in the center, to allow room for a line or two of quilting. Trace the feather motif onto the block and place a layer of batiste behind. Baste the outside edges of the feathers and along both sides of the channel. Quilt the interior lines which separate the feathers. Stuff the feather units through the batiste layer (Plates 3-23a and 3-23b). After the piece has been layered with batting and back, quilt around the outside edges and inside the channel to define the center line.

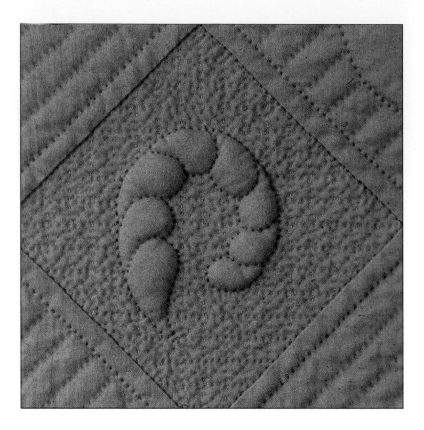

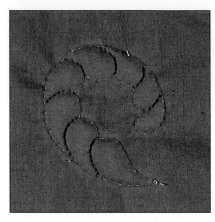

◁ *Plate 3-24.* Quilted fiddle-head feather.

△ *Plate 3-24a.* Single-sided feather, right side, with outline basted and interior lines quilted.

PROJECT 22: FIDDLEHEAD FEATHER — SINGLE-SIDED FEATHERS

By designing a feather motif with feathers on only one side of the vein line, the work can be approached as in technique #18 with the outside edges basted and the interior lines quilted through the batiste (Plates 3-24a and 3-24b). This narrower, single feather motif will not require extra quilting or tacking.

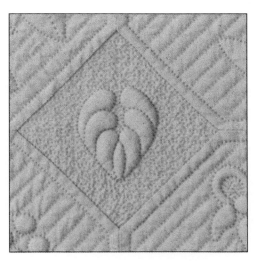

△ *Plate 3-24b.* Single-sided feather, wrong side, showing sections quilted and stuffed.

◁*Plate 3-24c.* Single-sided feathers.

ANITA SHACKELFORD: SURFACE TEXTURES

▷ *Plate 3-25.* Fiddlehead Feather with a corded spine.

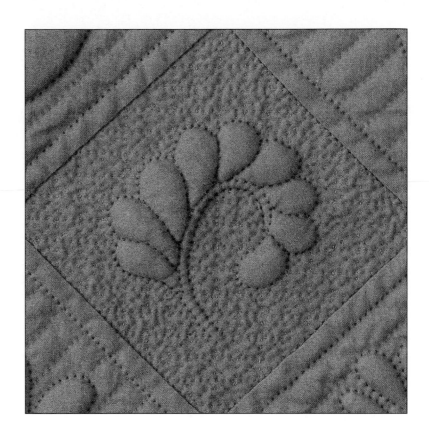

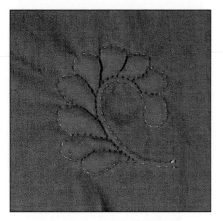

△ *Plate 3-25a.* Single-sided feather, right side, with outline basted and interior lines of feathers and spine quilted.

PROJECT #23: FIDDLEHEAD FEATHER WITH A CORDED SPINE

A single-sided feather can be made more complex by the addition of a corded spine. To prepare this motif for raised work, baste the outside edges of the feathers and quilt the interior lines through the batiste. Quilt the inner line of the channel and baste the outside line (Plates 3-25a and 3-25b). Stuff the feather units and cord the spine, as before. When the final quilting has been done through all layers, place a tacking stitch at the base of each feather to recess the vein line.

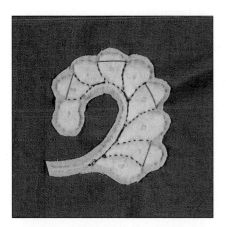

△ *Plate 3-25b.* Single-sided feather, wrong side, showing interior lines quilted. Channel is corded, feathers are stuffed.

▷ *Plate 3-25c.* Finished Feathered Pineapple block with single-sided feathers and corded spine.

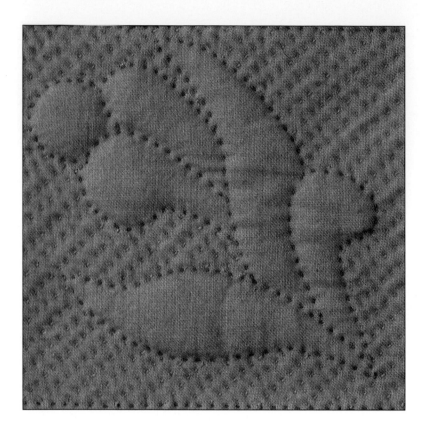

◁ *Plate 3-26. Padded Leaf and Feather motif.*

△ *Plate 3-26a. Basted and padded motif, right side.*

PROJECT #24: FEATHER AND LEAF DESIGN — PADDED AND QUILTED THROUGH ALL LAYERS

Small groupings of feathers and leaves may be handled as in technique #8 by cutting one layer of padding for the entire motif and quilting through the interior design lines to separate the individual elements (Plates 3-26a and 3-26b). Feathers worked in this way do not have as much loft as those stuffed individually, but these finish quickly and can be very graceful in design.

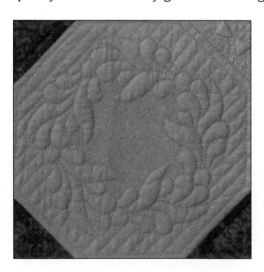

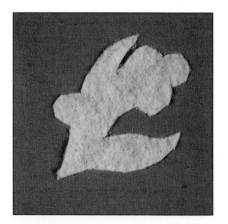

△ *Plate 3-26b. Basted and padded motif, wrong side.*

◁ *Plate 3-26c. Finished Leaf and Feather Wreath with interior lines quilted through all layers.*

▷ *Plate 3-27. Isolated Feathers.*

△ *Plate 3-27a. Basted and padded feathers, right side.*

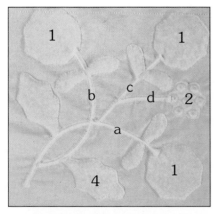

△ *Plate 3-27b. Basted and padded feathers, wrong side.*

△ *Plate 3-28. Sample block showing order of placement of pieces in complex design.*

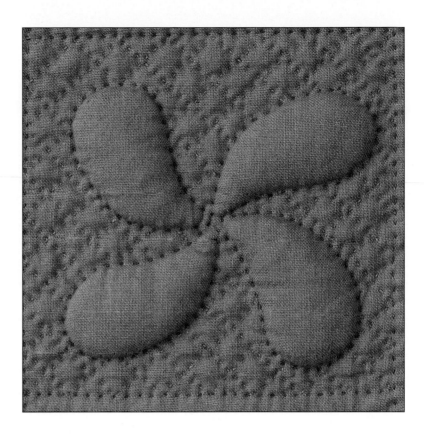

PROJECT #25: ISOLATED FEATHERS — STUFFED OR PADDED

Another solution for stuffed feathers is to redesign the motif, with isolated feathers, for ease in quilting around each one. For this approach the design may be backed with batiste, basted, and stuffed, as in technique #16.

Padded feathers are accomplished more quickly and are probably as effective visually if the batting has a good loft. The padding creates a smoother finish, with less distortion, especially if the design has many feathers. Pad and trim each feather as in technique #7 (Plates 3-27a and 3-27b). Try a sample each way to see which effect is most pleasing to you.

The patterns on pages 103 – 129 contain blocks which combine a variety of techniques in each design. For best effect, it is important to understand the order in which the work must progress when using all of the techniques together. The pieces must be layered in an order opposite from that of appliqué. In analyzing a pattern from the right side, those pieces which lie on top of another, or come forward in the design, must be applied first and those that lie behind, placed last. For example, in the large floral block in Plate 3-28, the pieces were added in this order:

1. large flowers   3. stems as: a, b, c, d
2. stuffed berries   4. leaves

Trim each piece as it is finished, before the next piece overlaps it.

CHAPTER 4

SUGGESTED PROJECTS

▷ *Plate 4-1.* *Technique Sampler 14" x 14". Made by the author, 1996.*

△ *Plate 4-2. "Little Water Lilies," 11¾" x 15", made by Ruth J. Kennedy, Fremont, Ohio, 1996. Small padded feather blocks alternate with foundation pieced flowers in a miniature quilt.*

△ *Plate 4-3.* "Bluebird," 16" x 16", 1996, made by the author for the NQA small quilt auction in memory of Palmer Clement. In the collection of Loretta Gelewicz.

QUILTS

The large blocks in the pattern section may be set together as octagons with small setting squares, as shown in "Through Rose Colored Glasses" on page 86 or as 9" squares for a whole-cloth look. The small technique blocks might be used together as a mini sampler (Plate 4-1).

You may choose to alternate one or many different raised work blocks in a patchwork setting, as in the friendship album quilt on page 85. Any of the designs in the pattern section can be combined with the album block for a similar friendship quilt.

The small blocks may be used in the same way with miniature patchwork (Plate 4-2). These little patterns will fit together easily with 3½" or 4" foundation-pieced blocks.

Use any of the designs as alternate blocks or in the background areas of an appliqué quilt of any size.

Some of the designs will also work well as appliqué patterns instead of background work (Plate 4-3).

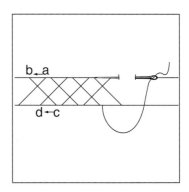

◁ *Plate 4-4. Kimmie coat, with padded Yukata designs, made by the author, 1989. Pattern by Deanna Powell.*

△ *Plate 4-5. Bishop's blouse with Marseilles-style corded design in yoke. Made by the author, 1996.*

CLOTHING

As shown in this kimono jacket (Plate 4-4), raised work may be added to garments in the same manner as in quilts, by cording, padding, or stuffing the design motifs. The garment can then be finished with a layer of batting added between the top and the lining and all of the layers quilted through.

Design options and approaches to the work may be different if the garment will not have batting or will not be quilted through extra layers. This white blouse with a corded yoke is a good example of raised work added to an area which will be faced or lined (Plate 4-5). The yoke section of the blouse was fully lined with batiste, onto which the Marseilles-style quilting pattern had been marked. After the channels were quilted and corded, the facing was added, and the blouse construction was finished as usual. No extra batting was added to this piece.

Padded work with a lining could be done in a similar manner. Mark the design onto the right side of the garment. Baste padding into place behind each design and trim it to fit. Or, mark the design on the wrong side of the garment and baste pre-cut padding into the design areas. Place a piece of interlining behind the design and quilt around each motif to hold it in place. Add the lining to finish the garment.

Another option would be to eliminate the interlining. Once the padding is basted into place, add the lining, or underneath piece of fabric as in a yoke, collar, or cuffs and quilt through the top and lining to hold the padding in place.

△ *Fig. 5. Herringbone stitch.*

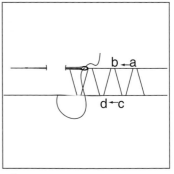

△ *Fig. 6. Running stitch.*

△ *Plate 4-6. Herringbone and running stitches, wrong side.*

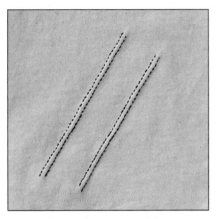

△ *Plate 4-7. Herringbone and running stitches create channels on the right side.*

△ *Plate 4-8. Seashell T-shirt made by the author, 1996.*

Stuffed work may also be put into an area of a garment which will be lined. There is one special advantage in stuffed work for clothing. Any style of design will work, even feather motifs stitched close together, since they will not need to be re-quilted. The design may be marked on the top or on the batiste layer. Quilt the two layers of fabric together and add the stuffing between the two layers. Trim away the excess batiste and finish the garment.

Unlined garments may be corded, padded, or stuffed.

Cording may be added to an unlined garment by using a stitching method similar to that described by Averil Colby in her 1971 book, *Quilting*. In this technique, a line of stitching is worked back and forth across the cording to hold it in place on the wrong side of the fabric. The first sample shows a line of cording secured with a herringbone stitch, worked from the wrong side, over the cording. To make a herringbone stitch, the needle points in the direction opposite the way the line is being worked and stitches are taken alternately above and below the line (Fig. 5, page 58).

A running stitch, with the needle pointing forward, may also be used. Again, work from the wrong side and alternate stitches above and below the line of cording (Fig. 6, page 58).

A herringbone stitch will create a line of cross stitches behind the cording, while a running stitch will produce a zigzag pattern.

Both produce a double line of stitches on the right side of the piece, which defines the corded channel (Plates 4-6 and 4-7).

For the best effect, it is important to keep the stitch length and tension even. Try both patterns to see which one is easier for you.

For an unlined padded garment, such as the T-shirt in Plate 4-8, mark the design on the front of the shirt and position pieces of batting behind each motif. Use basting stitches to define the outline of each motif and to hold the padding in place. Trim away the excess batting by cutting around each shape close to the basting line. Take special care in trimming behind a flexible fabric, such as a knit, so that you do not cut through the top layer. Place a full layer of batiste behind the design to prepare the piece for quilting. You will find that regular quilting thread is too fine and will fall down into the open texture of a T-shirt knit. Try quilting with a heavier thread such as 2 ply floss or #8 perle cotton or rayon for stitches which will have more texture and visual impact. When the quilting is finished, trim away the excess batiste.

To add stuffed work to an unlined garment, you may mark the design on the top or on the interlining. Quilt the two layers of fabric together and stuff the design areas from the wrong side. There is one disadvantage to stuffed work with no lining. Take care to make only tiny openings in the batiste as you add the stuffing. Larger holes may have to be stitched closed in order to hold the stuffing in place. For an unlined garment, cotton batiste or muslin may be a better choice for the interlining as it will not ravel.

Another example of adding raised work to ready-made clothing is this beautiful grape and vine design which Bonnie Browning added to a cotton turtleneck dress (Plate 4-9). Batiste was used as an inter-lining behind the bodice. The design was stitched with quilting thread and an outline embroidery stitch to add stability to the knit fabric. Acrylic yarn was used to cord the vines and fill the grapes.

Embroidery and stuffed work are a beautiful combination for clothing. The design for the quilted sweater front (Plate 4-10) was marked on the top layer. To prevent shadow-through with this white fabric, a full layer of batiste was placed behind, and the embroidery was worked through the top and batiste layers. After the design area was stuffed, a thin layer of batting and the lining were added and the background area was quilted through all layers.

MACHINE OPTIONS

The use of wash-out basting thread in the top and in the bobbin affords the additional option of machine basting for raised work, with no worry about how to remove the bobbin thread.

Stitching with a double needle makes it easy to prepare channels for corded work. Set the machine for a slightly longer stitch length and sew along the marked stem lines. Use a pin tuck foot and feed cording through the hole in the throat plate as you sew, stitching and filling the channel with cording at the same time. The zigzag stitch underneath will hold the cording in place until the quilt is lay-ered and quilted. If you are not comfortable with the idea of stitching and adding the cording in one step, the twin needle technique may also be used with a layer of batiste behind. These channels may be filled with a tapestry needle and yarn as previously described.

Plate 4-11 is a sampler of different size channels made with twin needles and corded with a variety of yarns.

Needle size 1.6, one strand of #5 Pearl Cotton
Needle size 2.0, one strand of acrylic baby yarn
Needle size 2.5, two strands of acrylic baby yarn
Needle size 3.0, one strand of acrylic rug yarn
Needle size 4.0, two strands of acrylic rug yarn

A size 3.0 needle and a 3-groove pin tuck foot were used to baste the cording into place on the miniature Colonial whole-cloth doll quilt (Plate 4-12, page 61).

Machine basting and wash-out thread may also be used for padded motifs. As with handwork, cut a piece of batting slightly larger than the design to be filled and position it behind the motif. Using an open toe foot or free motion, machine baste the batting into place, follow-ing the design marked on the top. If necessary, loosen the top tension to keep the thread from breaking. Stitch just inside the marked line, so as not to obscure the quilting line. Turn the piece over and trim the

△ **Plate 4-9.** *Grape design added to cotton knit dress by Bonnie Browning, Paducah, Kentucky, 1997.*

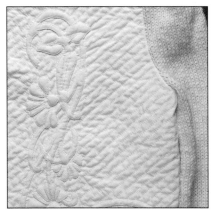

△ **Plate 4-10.** *Quilt sweater with embroidered and stuffed design, made by the author, 1997.*

Twin Needle Sizes

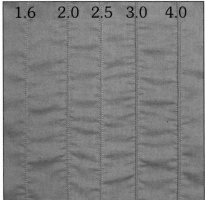

△ **Plate 4-11.** *Sampler of machine quilted and corded channels, made by Connie St. Clair, Helena, Ohio.*

△ *Plate 4-12.* Machine-basted channels.

△ *Plate 4-13.* Padding machine basted into place.

△ *Plate 4-14.* Colonial whole-cloth doll quilt, 16½" x 18", made by the author, 1996. Pattern credit: Mini Whole-cloth Designs by Pepper Cory.

batting close to the stitched line (Plate 4-13). The vase and the flowers were padded in this little quilt. When all of the cording and padding have been prepared, layer and quilt the piece as usual.

The Colonial whole cloth quilt was finished with outline quilting around all of the raised areas (Plate 4-14). The feather designs were quilted as they were marked and the piece was finished with ⅛" background quilting. There was no worry about quilting through the basting thread or removing the bobbin thread as it all dissolved when the piece was washed.

This sample demonstrates three levels of texture possible in a whole cloth quilt; the raised (padded and corded) work, the feathers which are filled with the single layer of batting in the main body of the quilt and the finely recessed background quilting.

HOME DEC/CHILDREN'S/CRAFTS

Children's quilts, craft projects, or decorative items provide other opportunities to use raised work techniques. The Northwoods Noel wall quilt was stitched by my daughter Jennifer. All of the printed motifs were padded using technique #7. Some areas, such as the little log cabin, were surface quilted as in technique #11, and then the piece was layered with batting and back. Jen has a fine quilting stitch and she did all of her detail and background quilting by hand (Plate 4-15).

Pre-printed fabrics are fun for children's quilts. If the piece will receive a great deal of use and wear, a fusible fleece might be a good idea for the padded work. Referring to the #7 padded technique on page 37, baste a layer or two of fleece and trim it to fit the design. Follow the manufacturer's directions to fuse the fleece to the quilt top. Layer the top with batting and a back, and quilt around all of the shapes and in the background as needed. Padding which has been

fused into place will add interesting texture to the surface of a child's quilt and produce a piece that will be durable enough to use.

△ *Plate 4-15.* Detail, Northwoods Noel, 24" x 28", made by Jennifer Shackelford Perdue, 1997.

CHAPTER 5

TEXTURED APPLIQUÉ

▷ *Plate 5-1. Appliquéd pineapple with corded channels and stuffed sections.*

△ *Plate 5-2. Appliquéd fruit bowl with a corded channel.*

△ *Plate 5-3. Detail showing cording used as center vein line in appliquéd Christmas cactus.*

Because raised work can be done between any two layers on a quilt, another option is possible. The two uppermost layers on a quilt where this work might be done are the appliqué pieces and the quilt block which lies behind.

Corded channels within an appliqué piece can add detail and interesting texture, as in the pineapple, fruit bowl, and Christmas cactus shown in Plates 5-1, 5-2, and 5-3. If you have an appliqué motif that you think would benefit from the addition of a corded line, begin by appliquéing the piece into place on the background. Quilt along both sides of the channel line, stitching the appliqué piece to the block. Cord the line by pulling the needle and yarn in and out through the background block, as shown (Fig. 7).

Stuffing can add full, rounded dimension to appliqué pieces such as fruit or flowers (Plate 5-4). To add stuffing under an appliqué motif, stitch the piece into place on the background block until only a small amount of edge remains unsewn. Take small pinches of stuffing and insert it through this opening until the piece is as full as you would like (Fig. 8).

Some motifs, such as the pineapple in Plate 5-1, will have sections

△ *Plate 5-4. Stuffing used to add texture to appliquéd grapes.*

△ *Fig. 7. Cording a channel within an appliqué piece.*

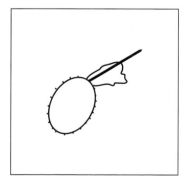

△ *Fig. 8. Inserting stuffing beneath appliqué piece.*

which are not accessible from the outside edge. In this situation, the stuffing can be added through small holes made in the background block behind each section.

Appliqué may also be padded to add a smoother, more natural raised appearance to some motifs such as fruit or animals (Plates 5-5 and 5-6). To pad an appliqué piece, begin by having seam allowances basted or pressed to the wrong side. Cut a layer or two of batting to fit beneath the appliqué shape and position both the padding and the appliqué piece on the background block. Appliqué around the piece as usual, tucking in the edges of the padding as necessary.

Because padded appliqué is made with the three layers of the appliqué piece, the batting, and the quilt block, these padded areas may be further textured with surface quilting. Think of the motif as a mini quilt on the surface of the background block and use quilting to add texture and detail to the piece (Plates 5-7 and 5-8).

Embroidery stitches worked through all three layers can add the texture of surface quilting, plus a color contrast to a padded piece (Plates 5-9 and 5-10). To begin, appliqué the motif with a layer of padding beneath it. Use a stem stitch in a matching or contrasting color of embroidery floss, or other special thread, to add detail lines. Make sure that the stitches penetrate all three layers to add depth and definition to the motif.

△ *Plate 5-5. Padded fruit included in "Harvest Wreath" made by the author, 1990.*

△ *Plate 5-6. Padded bluebirds from "The Shackelford Family Album Quilt," made by the author, 1989.*

△ *Plate 5-7. Padded cartouche with surface quilting, from "Hospitality," made by the author, 1993.*

△ *Plate 5-8. Blue vase with surface quilting, made by Glenda Clark, Marysville, Ohio.*

△ *Plate 5-9. Padded and embroidered morning glories from "Those Our Hearts Are Fondest Of," made by the author, 1992.*

△ *Plate 5-10. Padded and embroidered tulips from Follett House block, made by the author.*

CHAPTER 6

FINISHING

FINISHING

TRIMMING BLOCKS

After the surface work is finished, the blocks will need to be pressed and trimmed to size. Turn the blocks face down onto a heavy towel and press them from the wrong side to smooth and straighten them. You will probably find that some of the edges have been distorted by the raised work. Trimming the blocks at this stage will ensure that they will all be the same size and will fit together.

It is extremely important, when trimming blocks, to center the design so that the pattern repeats accurately block to block. Figures 9 and 10 show the design centered and not centered.

In order to guarantee that your designs will be properly centered, I recommend that you make a cutting template with a center mark and seam allowances added. In the pattern section of the book you will find templates with these markings included. The small squares should finish 3½". The larger patterns may be finished as an octagon or a square. Decide on the shape that you want for your quilt and make your template from clear plastic. It is important to include the seam allowance in the template. There is no need to mark the seam allowance line, but do place a mark in the center of the template. If you choose to set the quilt together with the large octagonal blocks and the small joining squares, you may find it helpful to mark the corners for more accurate joining of the set in pieces. Once the template is made, place it on the back of the pressed block, matching the center mark on the template to the center of the design as shown on the pattern. Draw around the template to mark the outside edge and mark the corner dots. Use scissors or a rotary cutter, and cut on the marked lines to trim each block to its proper size.

Study the finished designs for style and visual weight. Arrange the blocks in a balanced and pleasing set and stitch them together to make a full quilt top. Add borders if you like.

BATTING

When you are ready to select batting for the main body of the quilt, choose a regular or low loft cotton or polyester, as you prefer. Keep in mind that the batting must allow for fine quilting to recess the background, but it must have enough loft to show the texture produced by the quilting pattern. If you are working with a white top, check to see if the outline of the batiste shadows through. Cotton batting is not translucent like polyester and may prevent this shadowing problem.

BASTING

Raised work and fine background quilting can cause uneven shrinkage and distortion in a quilt top. To avoid this, it is important that the quilt is layed out straight and square and that the layers are basted

△ *Fig. 9. Block with design centered.*

△ *Fig. 10. Block with design not centered.*

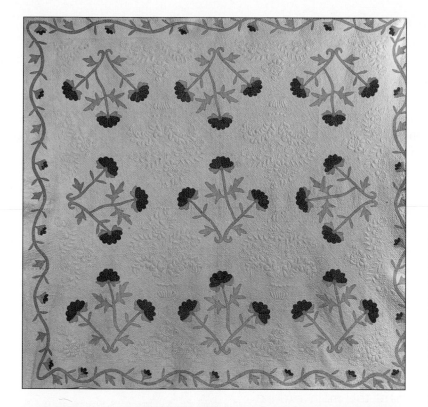

◁ **Plate 6-1.** *Red and green appliqué with stuffed work, c. 1860. Author's collection.*

securely to prevent any shifting. The most common, visually distracting error in a finished quilt happens when long seam lines are not straight.

Lay the quilt out on a flat surface. Smooth all of the layers one at a time, making sure that the edges are straight and the corners are square. Lay a long straight edge along each main seam in the quilt top and baste in the ditch to hold these long seams straight. A four foot straight edge and T-square will be very helpful during the basting process. Within this basted grid, secure each block approximately every 4" with other lines of stitching, safety pins, or tacks. Baste along the outside edges to ensure that they remain straight during the quilting process and to prevent shifting when the binding is applied.

QUILTING

Once the quilt is layered and prepared for quilting, it will probably need both outline quilting and background fill. At the far ends of the spectrum, Marseilles quilts with corded and stuffed work were outline quilted only. On early quilts of this style, motifs filled almost the entire ground, leaving no room for background quilting. As these designs became more open, some backgrounds were still left unquilted. Nineteenth century, American quilts were usually heavily quilted with background quilting lines often extending across the patchwork or appliqué (Plates 6-1 and 6-2).

△ **Plate 6-2.** *"Rising Sun," c. 1850–60, Cash family, Forsythe, GA. Collection of Bets Ramsey, Chattanooga, Tennessee.*

When finishing areas with raised work, quilt the design as marked, quilting around each part, just outside of the basting stitches. This final quilting is worked through all layers to hold the cording, padding, and stuffing in place. Some interior lines, such as leaf veins, will now be quilted through all of the layers. When quilting an embroidered piece, quilt just outside the embroidery line.

You may notice that in many of the samples, the quilting was done in color for emphasis (Plate 6-3). If the interior lines of a stuffed motif have been quilted in color, the final quilting around the outside edges will be done in the same color. When quilting with colored thread, bury the knots and tails inside stuffed areas for less chance of shadow through.

Remove the basting stitches as each area is quilted. Done a little at a time, this will not seem as big a job as it would if left until the end of the quilting, and you will be more likely to remove it all. After finishing the outline quilting, examine designs for those areas which might need tacking stitches within a motif in order to secure all of the layers.

Quilting stitches are used to hold the layers together and the filling in place. The quilting pattern does much more than that. The background quilting design should complement the main surface design. Fine quilting will recess the background and force unquilted or raised areas into high relief (Plates 6-4 and 6-5). Background quilting is most often worked in a variety of lines, grids, or echo patterns. The quilting pattern can be chosen to contrast or complement the main design. With raised work, the surrounding areas may require a generous amount of quilting to take up or shrink the background.

When planning your quilting pattern it is important to consider how the pattern will lie in relation to the grain line of the fabric. For best effect, plan to have as many long lines of quilting as possible, on the bias. Quilting on grain catches only the threads of the background fabric which run in one direction, that is, perpendicular to the quilted line. Small stitches which do not catch enough of the background may fall through between the threads, producing an uneven looking stitch length. The stitches may also skip back and forth across the weave and cause a crooked appearance to the line. Quilting on the bias catches both warp and weft threads keeping the quilting thread on top, and giving better support to the quilted line.

DESIGN CONSIDERATIONS

SCALE OF THE QUILTING MOTIF

When choosing a motif for quilting or raised work, look at the proportion of the design to the size of the block or border (Figs. 11 and 12, page 69). Does it fill the space? How much negative space is

△ **Plate 6-3.** *Rose motif quilted with colored thread.*

△ **Plate 6-4.** *Detail, border of "Sweetheart Rose" without background quilting.*

△ **Plate 6-5.** *Close background quilting pushes raised areas into high relief.*

△ **Fig. 11.** *Quilting pattern too small for space.*

△ **Fig.12.** *Quilting pattern fills space effectively.*

△ **Plate 6-6.** *¼" grid creates fine background for complex border quilting design.*

△ **Plate 6-7.** *½" lines fill area behind large appliquéd swags.*

left in the background? Keep in mind that "whatever you stuff, you don't have to stipple."

Consider the proportion of the background quilting to the main design element, whether it be appliqué, raised work, or a quilting design. The fine detail of the border quilting design in "Those Our Hearts Are Fondest Of" required a ¼" grid to set it off (Plate 6-6). Lines ½" apart provided enough background support and texture for the large appliquéd swags in "Hospitality" (Plate 6-7).

Also consider the scale of the quilting design for the size of the quilt. Miniature quilts will require smaller motifs and very fine background quilting (Plate 6-8).

Choose a style of background quilting that will work best technically and visually with the main design elements. Background lines should contrast in some way with the lines of the foreground. For example, in choosing a background for a pineapple design, you can

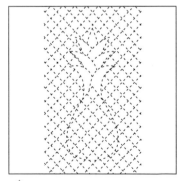

△ **Fig. 13.** *Design of pineapple is lost in large grid.*

◁**Plate 6-8.** *Stipple quilting and ¼" lines in "Miniature Baltimore Album," 23" x 23", made by the author, 1995.*

see that a large grid may fall too much in line with the grid of the fruit (Fig. 13, page 69), while an echo pattern causes the design of the leaves to be lost (Fig. 14). Parallel lines or a finer grid may be better choices here (Figs. 15 and 16).

Background quilting should relate in mood to the style of the quilt, such as ornate quilting with Victorian designs or simpler lines behind folk art appliqué.

Sometimes background quilting can be inspired by or dictated by the design in the fabric. If your background fabric is printed with a grid, swirls, or a basket-weave pattern, let those lines determine the mood and pattern of your quilting (Plate 6-9).

Background quilting may be inspired by, or an extention of, the appliqué design. Study the motifs which make up the appliqué design and see which ones might be adapted to use as quilting designs (Plate 6-10 and 6-11).

For best visual interest, think about using straight line or grid quilting behind curves, flowing patterns with floral appliqué, as above, curves or feathers alternated with patchwork, and straight background quilting lines in opposition to the line of the design motif. The quilted border in Plate 6-12 shows a contrast in both scale and style of design with ½" grid worked

△ *Fig. 14. Leaves are lost in echo quilting.*

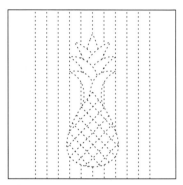

△ *Fig. 15. Good contrast with parallel lines.*

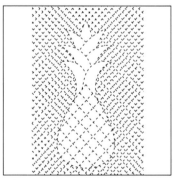

△ *Fig. 16. Good contrast with small grid.*

▷ *Plate 6-9. Quilting lines follow printed grid in fabric.*

△ *Plate 6-10.* Bluebirds from *"Those Our Hearts are Fondest Of."* Background quilting repeats branches, leaves, and tendrils.

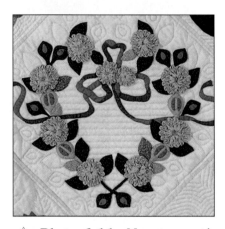

△ *Plate 6-11. Heart wreath and ruched flowers from "Those Our Hearts are Fondest Of." Buds, leaves, and ribbon motifs repeated as quilting designs.*

△ *Plate 6-12. Grid behind feather shows good contrast.*

△ *Plate 6-13. A sampler of background quilting patterns.*

behind a larger running feather.

TEXTURE

When deciding on a background fill, consider the amount of stitching time it will require, plus the density of pattern and the visual texture desired in the finished piece. Keep in mind also that the raised effect of padded and stuffed work becomes increasingly more pronounced with increasing density of the background quilting pattern.

Small green leaf blocks were stitched as a sampler of background quilting patterns to show a variety of styles, density of pattern, and visual textures (Plate 6-13).

Background Quilting Methods

Perhaps the simplest background pattern is composed of straight, parallel lines. Lines may be marked or the spacing may be measured with tape. Use the method you prefer and the one which will guarantee that the lines remain parallel.

1. ½" line

Plate 6-14 shows lines spaced ½" apart. Begin this pattern by quilting a  line from corner to corner in the block. Mark parallel lines on both sides of this diagonal line or, if using tape, reposition it to lie beside the line just quilted and add another line of quilting, parallel to the first. Notice that, in the leaf block, the quilting lines fall in line with the angle of the leaf.

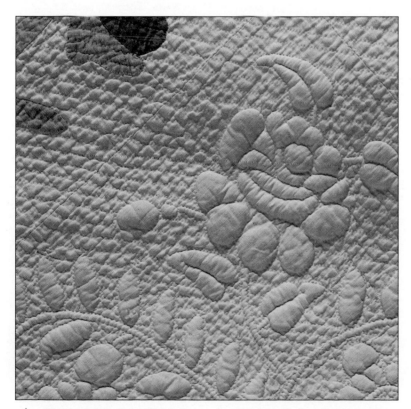

△ *Plate 6-14. Parallel lines in background of antique quilt.*

2. ½" grid

On the second sample, lines with the same ½" spacing were repeated in the opposite direction to form a grid pattern. Although this block has twice as much quilting, and the background is more recessed and controlled, it still has a very open look. A ½" grid works well behind a quilted feather wreath in this late nineteenth century Feathered Star quilt (Plate 6-15).

3. ¼" line

For a finer background line pattern, use ¼" quilter's masking tape or marked lines, as in the first sample, to quilt parallel lines with ¼" spacing. Note that in this block, the lines run in contrast to the angle of the leaf.

While this pattern appears to fill the background much more completely, it is actually the same amount of stitching as the ½" grid (2) above. Think of it as quilting the ½" spacing and then a second set of lines parallel, or in between, instead of across the first set. This simple variation creates a very different look with the same amount of work (Plate 6-16).

△ **Plate 6-15.** *½" grid background in antique quilt. "Feathered Star," c. 1870. Made by Mincks family, Bowling Green, Ohio. Author's collection.*

△ **Plate 6-16.** *Background quilting with ¼" line pattern. Detail of rose block from "Friendship," made by the author, 1996.*

4. ¼" echo

For a variation in this spacing, try quilting a ¼" echo pattern. Echo quilting can be done by eye. As an alternative, the pattern can be marked by putting your fabric marking pencil into a compass set for ¼" spacing. Use the point of the compass to follow the outline and trace around the design, adding concentric rings of quilting lines until the space is filled (Plate 6-17).

I measured the thread that I used when quilting the samples of the ¼" line and ¼" echo patterns and found that they required the same amount of thread. Therefore, patterns 2, 3, and 4 were all completed with the same investment of time.

△ **Plate 6-17.** *Background quilting with ¼" echo pattern. Family hand prints from "Those Our Hearts Are Fondest Of."*

5. ¼" grid

You can create an even finer background quilting pattern with ¼" grid. Begin with ¼" spacing of parallel lines and then repeat the pattern in the opposite direction. This third possible style with ¼" spacing, creates a somewhat denser look, but with twice the work of the others (Plate 6-18).

△ **Plate 6-18.** *Detail, ¼" grid from "Hospitality."*

6. ⅛" line

By repeating the second set of lines parallel to, instead of across, the ¼" spaced lines (3), you can create  a much finer background fill, approaching stipple. Simply add another line, by eye, in between each of the lines already in place. The same holds true here as in the comparison of ½" grid and ¼" line patterns. This ⅛" spacing is a very different look and much finer texture (Plate 6-19), but with the same amount of work as ¼" grid.

When adding a line, by eye, to a space which begins on an angle, it is sometimes difficult to know where to begin. Holding your needle or thread in the center of the space will help you to see the placement of the next line (Fig. 17).

When planning a background quilting pattern, be aware that some shrinkage and distortion may be caused by quilting long lines diagonally in only one direction.

△ **Plate 6-19.** *Background of a doll quilt with ⅛" line pattern.*

STIPPLE QUILTING

Stippling is an art term that is defined as producing a pattern or texture by means of small points or dots. You will find stippling used in painting, metal work (Plate 6-20), leather tooling, and quilting.

Stipple quilting will add the very finest background texture to your quilts. Most often the exquisite background quilting on antique quilts was done in a straight line pattern, although we sometimes find an echo or somewhat random pattern.

THE PROCESS

The texture of stipple quilting is created by the number of closely placed stitches and the small amounts of fabric that stand up between them, not by making tighter than normal quilting stitches. Do not pull the stitches in order to create texture. This will cause distortion of the quilt surface. The tension of the quilting stitch should be enough to squeeze the layers together, but not so much that it draws or gathers the fabric along the quilting line.

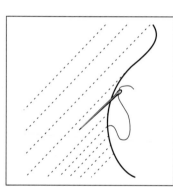

△ **Fig. 17.** *Repeating parallel lines creates ⅛" background fill.*

△ **Plate 6-20.** *Brass door sign with stipple background. Photo by author.*

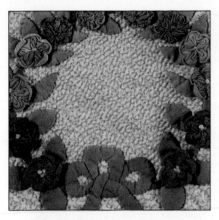

△ *Plate 6-21. Stipple quilting on a fine print background.*

△ *Plate 6-22. Straight line stipple quilting used to fill Christmas Cactus Wreath from "Those Our Hearts Are Fondest Of."*

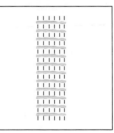

△ *Fig. 18. Ridges form perpendicular to lines of quilting.*

△ *Fig. 19. When stitches are offset, ridges become ripples.*

Thread

Thread for stipple quilting should match the color of the background, unless another effect is desired. Keep in mind that for background work, we want to see the texture produced by the stitching, not the individual stitches themselves.

If your stitches are not as small as you would like, consider using a finer thread for the stipple quilted areas. Because there will be so many stitches in the piece, a heavy thread is not needed for strength. A finer thread will make your stitches appear more delicate, as well. Try a practice piece with a sewing-weight thread or a machine embroidery-weight thread to see the difference.

Fabric

Stipple quilting on cotton creates beautiful texture as the fabric wrinkles between the stitches. You will also find that the stitches create more visual texture on muslin or plain colors. Most often, the texture of fine quilting will be lost on a busy background print, but may work well on a fine print which reads almost as a solid from a distance (Plate 6-21).

Because stipple quilting will cause more shrinkage than normal background quilting, it is important to consider the balance of placement in the quilt. Fine quilting should be used as an accent in small areas, or should be used equally throughout the quilt. The quilt should be secured in a hoop or frame during quilting in order to lessen the shrinkage in closely quilted areas. There may be some advantage to quilting in a hoop to control the tension within a small area of the quilt as the stipple quilting is being done.

You will also find that heavily quilted areas are somewhat stiff and have less drape than those with less quilting. This causes a problem in garments more often than in bed quilts or wall quilts.

STIPPLE PATTERNS

STRAIGHT LINE STIPPLE

A straight line style of stipple quilting was often used in nineteenth century quilts, and is certainly the simplest to work. The texture of fabric when it is so closely quilted can obscure the straight line quilting pattern and create a much more complex appearance (Plate 6-22).

Working stitches through multiple layers of fabric causes a small ridge to form between the stitches within each line of quilting. When straight lines of stitching are placed side by side, the texture created by these little ridges actually forms perpendicular to the stitched line. The stipple pattern will take on a different texture depending on whether the stitches from one line to the next are regularly or irregularly placed (Figs. 18 and 19). Although I never concentrate on whether my stitches are side by side or offset, it is interesting to understand how this pattern develops.

To try a sample of straight line stipple quilting, begin by quilting parallel lines ¼" apart. Quilt again between the lines, placing two additional lines in each space for a final spacing of 12 lines to the inch (Fig. 20). If you are quilting 10–12 stitches per inch, you will be putting approximately 120–144 stitches into each square inch of the quilt (Plates 6-23 and 6-24).

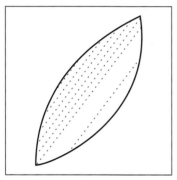

△ **Fig. 20.** *Quilt two more lines in each ¼" channel for straight line stipple pattern.*

△ **Plate 6-24.**
Straight line stipple.

GRID STIPPLE

A grid stipple pattern (Plates 6-25 and 26) requires the same amount of work as the straight line pattern above, but lines of quilting run in three different directions. Begin with

△ **Plate 6-23.** *Straight line stipple used as background in Evergreen Wreath.*

△ **Plate 6-25.** *Grid stipple quilting used to fill Redbud Wreath from "Those Our Hearts Are Fondest Of."*

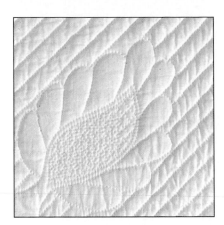

Plate 6-26. Grid stipple pattern.

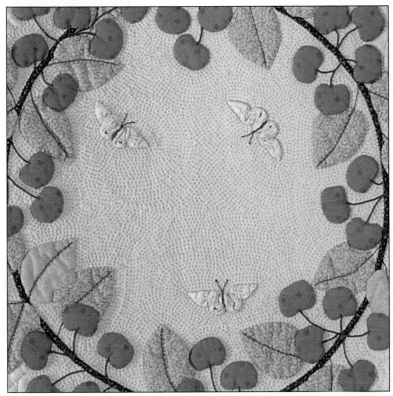

△ *Plate 6-27.* Echo stipple quilting used to fill Cherry Wreath from "Those Our Hearts Are Fondest Of."

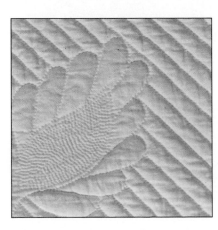

Plate 6-28. Echo stipple pattern.

¼" spacing of lines in two directions to form a grid. Add the third line, on the diagonal or in a zigzag pattern, through the little squares of

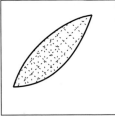

△ *Fig. 21.*

the grid (Fig. 21). You will find that although this pattern has a somewhat random look, it is very structured with controlled spacing and is easy to accomplish (Plate 6-26).

If you don't like working with marked lines or tape for these linear patterns, try quilting closely spaced lines or crosshatch by eye. Some irregularities will add to the textured effect.

ECHO STIPPLE

Both the line and grid patterns are measured and logical. The echo pattern is worked by eye, with no measuring and no marks, but it is still a very easy progression, with the pattern building on what is already there (Plates 6-27 and 6-28). If you have worked the straight line stipple pattern, your eye should be trained to ½" spacing. Simply follow the outline of the quilted motif or the appliqué, working around and around, until the space is filled (Fig 22). Be careful not to work the lines too close together. Remember that, in the end, it is not the stitches themselves but the texture of the

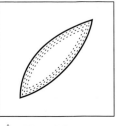

△ *Fig. 22.*

fabric between the stitches that is important. It is necessary to leave a small amount of fabric to stand up between the rows of stitching in order to create the desired texture.

When using echo stipple to fill a space, begin at the outside of the area to be filled and quilt following the edge of the design. Work toward the inside placing adjacent rows of quilting ⅟₁₂" away from the previous line. As areas of quilting begin to touch, or close, continue filling the available space. Some areas will become isolated; fill them in the same way from the outside to the inside. As these smaller areas close, you may worry that there is too much fabric remaining in the center. Just continue quilting, and you will find that this fullness will be taken up with the many stitches.

The echo pattern works in much the same way for filling a background space. The raised work or appliqué should be outline quilted in the ditch as closely as possible. Begin echoing the shape with another line of quilting ⅟₁₂" away and continue around the motif (Fig. 23). You may choose to work in concentric shapes or spirals; the finished effect will be the same.

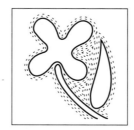

△ **Fig. 23.**

Echo quilting is easier to see with a simple shape such as the leaf in Plate 6-29, but can become repetitive and boring with simple lines or large open spaces to fill as in the background of the pineapple in Plate 6-30.

An echo pattern is much more interesting visually when used around a complex design which changes direction often, or in small spaces that close quickly.

SERPINTINE STIPPLE

Another curvilinear pattern can be created with a line which repeats its own shape rather than that of the appliqué or quilting design (Fig. 23a). Begin by drawing an undulating line in any area of the background. Fill the background with an echo stipple, repeating the shape of the original line and using the same ⅟₁₂" spacing as before.

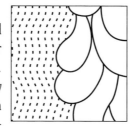

△ **Fig. 23a.**

RANDOM STIPPLE

Line, grid, and echo patterns are all linear and logical with controlled spacing. A random pattern is none of those things. Worked completely by eye, the pattern is irregular, changing direction every one, two, or three stitches (Plate 6-31). Random stipple looks like a wandering path when drawn, but because hand quilting is a broken line, the finished effect appears to be a grouping of random stitches.

△ **Fig. 24.**

Several problems seem common when working with a random pattern. There is no basic structure or

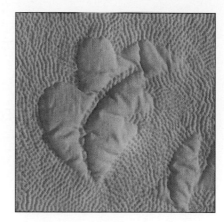

△ **Plate 6-29.** *Leaf sample with echo stipple background. Note corners finished in different ways.*

△ **Plate 6-30.** *Echo pattern may be too repetitive in large open space.*

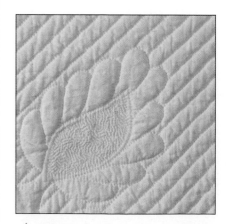

△ **Plate 6-31.** *Random stipple pattern.*

△ **Plate 6-32.** *Random stipple quilting used to fill Grape Wreath from "Those Our Hearts Are Fondest Of."*

spacing to this pattern, so it is easy to place stitches too close together. Be sure to leave approximately the same space as before in between the stitches. A random pattern is probably most effective if the spacing of some of the stitches varies slightly from $\frac{1}{8}$" to $\frac{1}{12}$" apart. Be careful not to pull stitches too tightly; this seems to be more of a problem with the constant change of direction in the random pattern. Also, if you find in your everyday quilting that your first stitch is larger than the others, this problem will be even more obvious in a random pattern since you are working with only one or two stitches at a time. Make a special effort to make that first stitch smaller. A larger stitch can be very evident, while a smaller one will not show nearly as much.

There may be a tendency to fall into a more regular echo pattern when quilting across a large space. To avoid this, divide the space, and work the random stipple pattern in one small area at a time (Fig. 25).

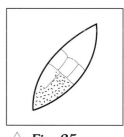

△ **Fig. 25.**

A random pattern has a special advantage for filling irregular spaces where long lines or grids would be impractical (Plate 6-34). Simply begin working in one corner and let the pattern grow in any direction until it has filled the space.

△ **Plate 6-33.** *Random stipple used in background space in "Hospitality."*

△ **Plate 6-34.** *Random stipple pattern works well in an irregular space.*

Random stipple also develops small secondary pattern groupings as stitches fall in line with each other. These little ripples add a great deal to the visual effect of the random pattern (Plate 6-35).

ROSETTE STIPPLE

Irma Gail Hatcher of Conway, Arkansas, is well known for her award-winning appliqué and hand quilting. When Irma Gail made her beautiful "Conway Album" quilt, she used a fine rosette pattern in the stipple quilted areas. She says she developed this pattern because she wanted to be able to quilt without markings and was looking for an alternative to a true random stipple. This rosette pattern begins with a small center circle and spirals, forming small petals (Fig. 26). The rosette pattern allows Irma Gail to follow a logical progression, but the finished appearance has the slightly irregular spacing of a random stipple pattern. Clusters of small flowers set close together require only a few stitches to fill the space between them (Plate 6-36).

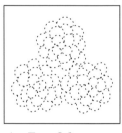
△ **Fig. 26.**

TEARDROP STIPPLE

Irma Gail Hatcher has also developed a different style of stipple quilting for filling a space. She begins by dividing the area into smaller sections using a curvilinear pattern such

△ *Plate 6-35. Random stipple can form beautiful secondary patterns. Detail from Evergreen and Chickadee Wreath, made by the author, 1994.*

△ *Plate 6-36. Rosette stipple pattern. "Conway Album (I'm Not from Baltimore)," 1991, 90" x 90", Irma Gail Hatcher. AQS Gingher Award for Hand Workmanship, 1994. Collection of the Museum of the American Quilter's Society.*

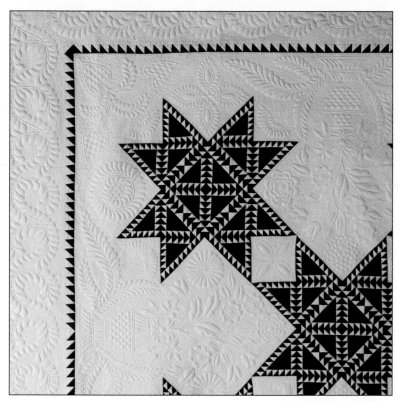

△ *Fig. 27.*

as a tear-drop shape and then echo quilts closely to fill each one, continuing until the entire space has been quilted (Fig. 27).

△ *Plate 6-37. Machine stippled background. Ohio Bride's Quilt, Debra Wagner, 81" x 81", 1989. Collection of the Museum of the American Quilter's Society.*

MACHINE STIPPLE

Debra Wagner of Cosmos, Minnesota, has created several award-winning quilts which feature stuffed work and fine background quilting done by machine. For her machine stipple quilting, Deb prefers to use a fine cotton thread that matches the color of the quilt top. She defines machine stipple quilting as extremely close, tiny, free-motion stitches. The stipple patterns that Deb prefers to use are a meandering line or close lines of echo quilting (Plate 6-37). She says that small, random, free-motion designs are the easiest and fastest to stitch and do not require marking or the challenge of following a drawn line.

I choose quilting patterns according to the space to be filled and the desired effect. Stipple quilting recesses the background and also adds beautiful texture to the piece. The random stipple pattern is my favorite to work and also my favorite in finished appearance. Over a large quilted surface, I enjoy using a combination of several patterns and spacing for the most depth and surface texture. Combining several quilting designs also adds variety and visual interest to the quilt (Plate 6-38).

All stippling requires approximately the same amount of time. Perhaps a random pattern takes slightly longer because of decisions about the placement of stitches, but it becomes quicker with a little experience. I have never been concerned about how much time I spend in quilting a piece. On occasion, I have gone back and added more quilting to a piece that did not seem finished, but I have never regretted the amount of time spent.

△ *Plate 6-38. A combination of several patterns and spacing create depth and texture in center of "Hospitality."*

GALLERY

"Hospitality," 84" x 84", 1993, made by the author.
A medallion arrangement combining appliqué and raised work. The appliquéd pineapples are raised with both corded and stuffed work. The small cartouches, appliquéd in a medium value, are padded and surface quilted to add detail. The small shells are stuffed appliqué or whole cloth, and the large cartouches are padded work added behind the quilt top. The background quilting in this quilt includes ½" lines and grids, ¼" lines and grids, and both echo and random stipple. Winner of Mary Krickbaum Award for Excellence in Hand Quilting, NQA, 1993.

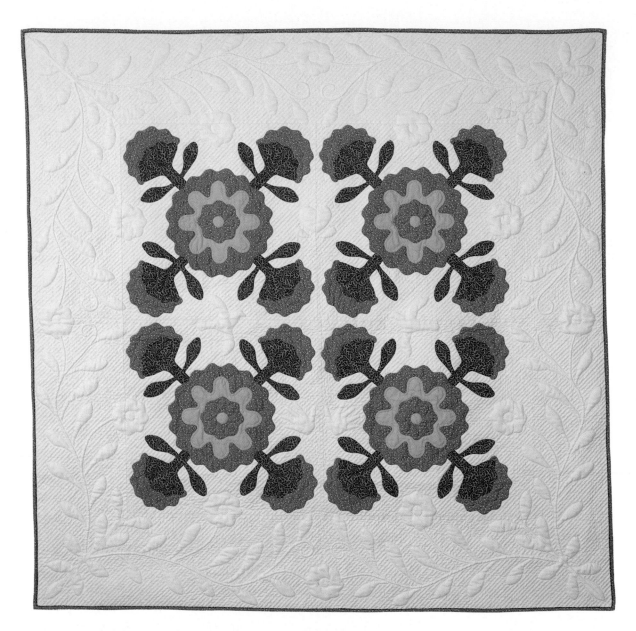

"Sweetheart Rose," *51" x 51", 1997, made by the author.*
A legacy quilt made for my granddaughter, Amber, who shares my middle name of Rose. The quilt is hand appliquéd with corded and padded work in the background and the borders. The small hands are from tracings of Amber's hands at six months of age. The background is quilted in diagonal lines ¼" apart.

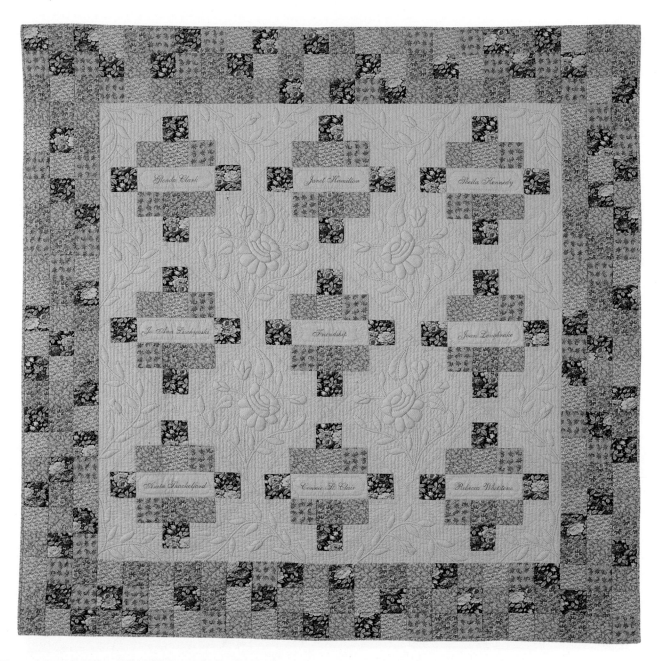

"Friendship," 47" x 47", 1996, made by the author.
Nine traditional Album blocks record the names of friends who have studied and worked together for many years. Alternate plain blocks and side triangles are filled with a rose motif done in corded and stuffed work. The background is quilted in straight lines ¼" apart.

"Through Rose Colored Glasses," *65" x 65", 1997, made by the author.*
This sampler quilt is a combination of the patterns included in the technique section and pattern section of this book. The blocks are set together as whole cloth and framed with a large Provencal-style border.

"Victorian Fantasy of Feathers and Lace," 89" x 100", 1986, made by Beverly Mannisto Williams, Cadillac, Michigan. Collection of the Museum of the American Quilter's Society.

A graceful combination of feather plumes, shells, and flowers are all created with cording. The main designs are quilted in brown thread, and the background lines and grids are quilted in an off-white color to match the background. The quilt is finished with a beautiful edging, which displays Beverly's other talent, hand-made bobbin lace.

ANITA SHACKELFORD: SURFACE TEXTURES

"Spring's Symphony," *62" x 82", 1992, made by Jane Holihan, Walworth, New York. Jane Holihan is well known for her beautiful, appliqué quilts which usually include quilted feathers or other subtle raised work designs. This quilt is a splendid example of raised work incorporated into the total design. Softly stuffed feathers intertwine with appliqué motifs throughout the quilt. Background spaces are filled with straight line and grid quilting.*

"Ohio Bride's Quilt," 81" x 81", 1989, made by Debra Christine Wagner, Cosmos, Minnesota. Collection of the Museum of the American Quilter's Society.

Debra's quilt shows the beauty of a crisp blue and white quilt accented with raised work in the background and borders. Five, perfectly pieced, feathered stars are surrounded by an assortment of stuffed floral and feather motifs. The background is entirely machine stipple quilted.

"Hanging Gardens," c. 1835, New England. Mountain Mist collection, Cincinnati, Ohio.
A large cornucopia filled with fruit and flowers is bordered by a feather swag. All of the motifs were raised with corded and stuffed work, and the background quilting was done in diagonal lines. Originally white, this quilt was overdyed a coral color sometime in the mid-twentieth century. Mountain Mist first offered a pattern for this quilt in the 1950's.

*"**Rose Wreath,**" 86½" x 90", third quarter, nineteenth century. Possibly from New York State. Collection of Sara Rhodes Dillow, Fremont, Nebraska.*
This beautiful example of a textured appliqué quilt includes roses and star-shaped flowers detailed with surface quilting and stuffed in sections.

"Medallion Floral Wreath," 85" x 95", third quarter, nineteenth century. Collection of Sara Rhodes Dillow. Stuffing was used to raise both the flowers and the small yellow circles which form the swag border of this medallion style quilt.

ANITA SHACKELFORD: SURFACE TEXTURES

Wedding gown.
Jacqueline Janovsky, Annapolis, Maryland, chose a duponi silk when she made this beautiful wedding gown for her daughter Amy. Motifs taken from lace were adapted to fit the front and back of the bodice. The design was marked onto an interlining, hand quilted from the wrong side with silk thread, and corded with polyester yarn.

CHAPTER 7

PATTERN SECTION

△ *Plate 7-1. Author's grandmother's wedding bracelet used as a design source.*

△ *Plate 7-2. Bracelet design interpreted in "The Shackelford Family Album Quilt" with embroidery and padding.*

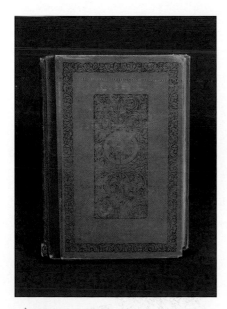

△ *Plate 7-3. Book cover as design source.*

DESIGN INSPIRATION

When looking for patterns for raised work, there is much available to serve as inspiration. When I made "The Shackelford Family Album Quilt," I wanted to include as many personalized designs as possible. Because my Grandmother's wedding bracelet has always been an important piece of jewelry in my family, the design was adapted to hold our family name (Plates 7-1 and 7-2). Both the lettering and the cartouche were embroidered with #5 perle cotton and padded from behind with two layers of batting. Random stipple quilting adds texture to the background spaces.

When I was ready to add a border to "Those Our Hearts Are Fondest Of," I wanted a design that would look like a carved, Victorian picture frame. The cover of an old McGuffey Reader provided a border quilting pattern with just the right look (Plates 7-3 and 7-4).

In searching for a design which would allow me to incorporate several raised work techniques, I found a silver tea tray which had belonged to my husband's grandmother (Plate 7-5). Although the central motif does not contain pineapples, I knew that they would fit nicely into the design that was there. The design of the tray was enlarged to create a medallion for a full-size quilt (Plate 7-6). The swag border was added next and then parts of the central design were adapted, changed in size, and rearranged to fill the spaces between the central motif and the borders. The pineapples were appliquéd with corded and stuffed work added

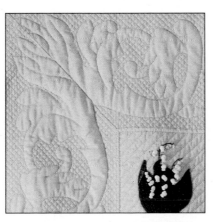

△ *Plate 7-4. Design from book cover used as quilting design in border of "Those Our Hearts Are Fondest Of."*

△ *Plate 7-5. Silver tea tray as design inspiration.*

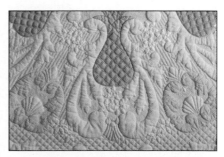

△ *Plate 7-6. Designs from tea tray used as center medallion of "Hospitality."*

between the appliqué and the quilt top. The small cartouches and shells, appliquéd in a medium value, are either padded or stuffed and the large cartouches are padded work added behind the quilt top. The background quilting in this quilt includes ½" line and grid, ¼" line and grid, and both echo and random stipple.

Mary Core of Huntington, West Virginia, used a serving tray that belonged to her mother-in-law as inspiration for an all white, corded, and stuffed quilt which she calls "Freda's Tray" (Plate 7-7, page 96) The quilt was a second place winner at the 1993 AQS show.

Look around, at art, at architecture, and at everyday household items. You will find wonderful designs in metal or plaster ceilings, carved wooden panels, doors, picture frames, furniture, wallpaper, wrought iron, book bindings, pottery, painted dishes, silver, theorem paintings, leaded glass, and grave stones. Be inspired; adapt designs from other sources as quiltmakers have always done and use them to add beautiful surface texture to your quilts.

△ **Plate 7-7.** *"Freda's Tray," 72" x 88", 1993. Mary Lenhart Core.*

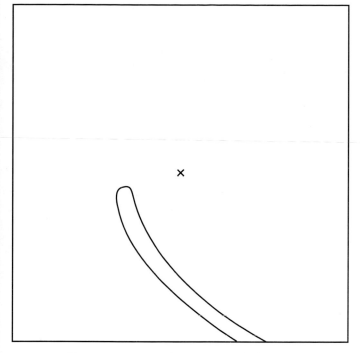

PROJECT #1, PAGE 31 —
FLOWER STEM

PROJECT #2, PAGE 32 —
DAISY

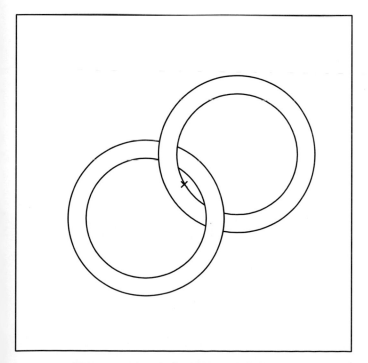

PROJECT #3, PAGE 33 —
RINGS

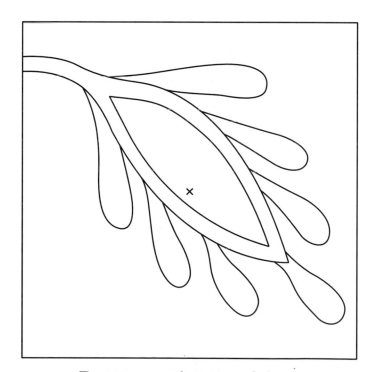

PROJECT #4, PAGE 34 —
TEAR DROP FLOWER

PROJECT #5, PAGE 35 —
CHERRIES

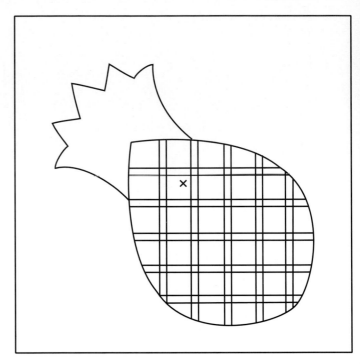

PROJECT #6, PAGE 36 —
PINEAPPLE

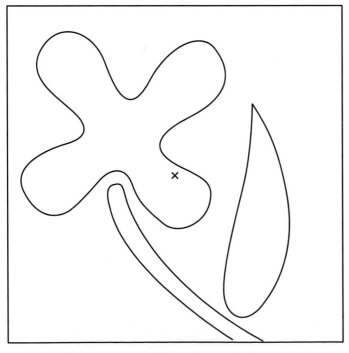

PROJECT #7, PAGE 37 —
FOUR PETAL FLOWER

PROJECT #8, PAGE 38 —
OAK LEAF

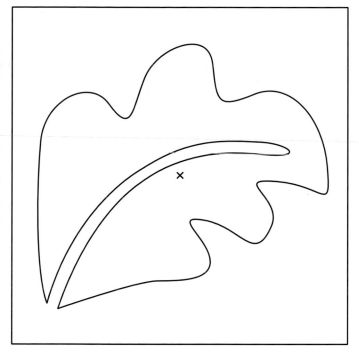

PROJECT #9, PAGE 39 —
LEAF

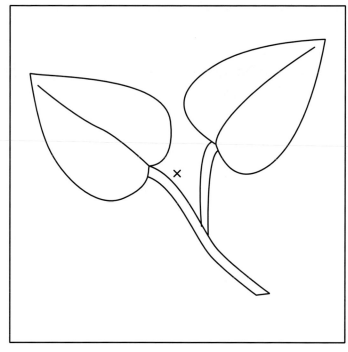

PROJECT #10, PAGE 40 —
TWO LEAVES

NO PATTERN PROVIDED FOR PROJECT #12.

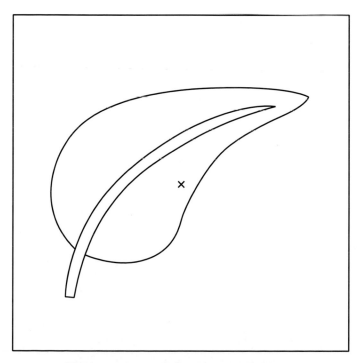

PROJECT #11, PAGE 41 —
LEAF – CORDED VEIN

PROJECT #13, PAGE 43 —
LAUREL LEAVES

ANITA SHACKELFORD: SURFACE TEXTURES

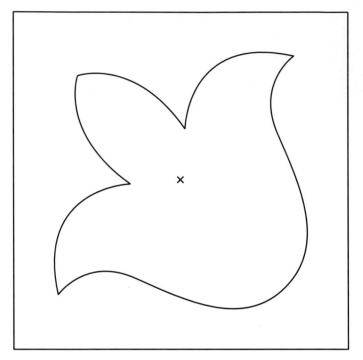

PROJECT #14, PAGE 44 —
TULIP

PROJECT #15, PAGE 45 —
SIX PETAL FLOWER

PROJECT #16, PAGE 47 —
SUNFLOWERS

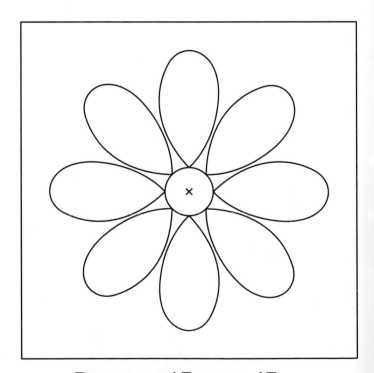

PROJECT #17, PAGE 47 —
EIGHT PETAL FLOWER

PROJECT #18, PAGE 48 —
ROSE BUD

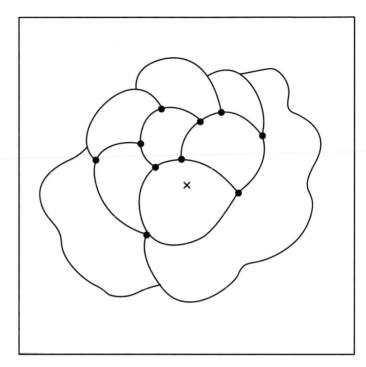

PROJECT #19, PAGE 49 —
PEONY

PROJECT #20, PAGE 50 —
FEATHERS

PROJECT #21, PAGE 51 —
FEATHERS

PROJECT #22, PAGE 52 —
FIDDLEHEAD

PROJECT #23, PAGE 53 —
FIDDLEHEAD WITH CORDED SPINE

PROJECT #24, PAGE 54 —
FEATHER AND LEAF

PROJECT #25, PAGE 55 —
ISOLATED FEATHERS

ANITA SHACKELFORD: SURFACE TEXTURES

DAISY

#2, page 32, corded with full interlining

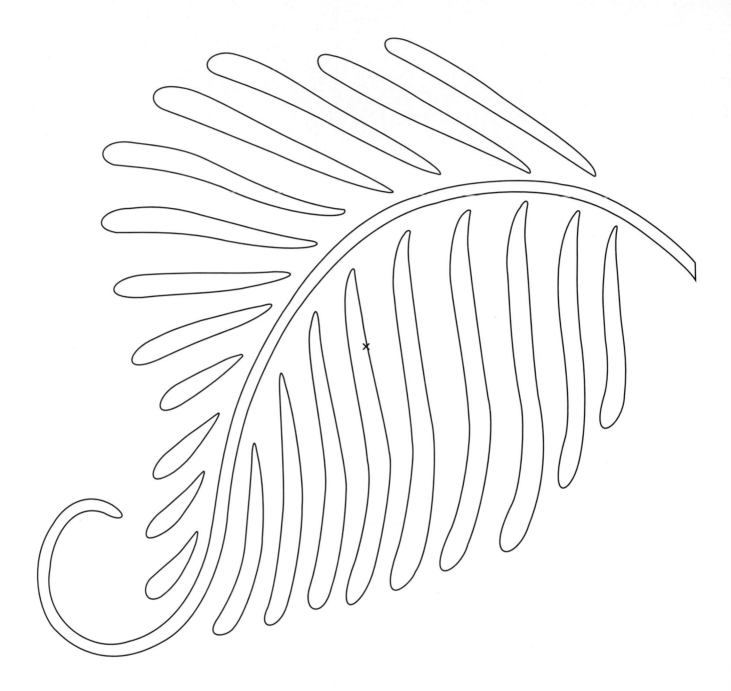

FERN

#2, PAGE 32, corded with full interlining

CARTOUCHE

#7, page 37, padded

OAK LEAVES

#8, page 38, padded with interior lines
quilted through all layers

ANITA SHACKELFORD: SURFACE TEXTURES

TULIPS

Tulips — #7, page 37, padded
Stems — #5, page 35, branching stems

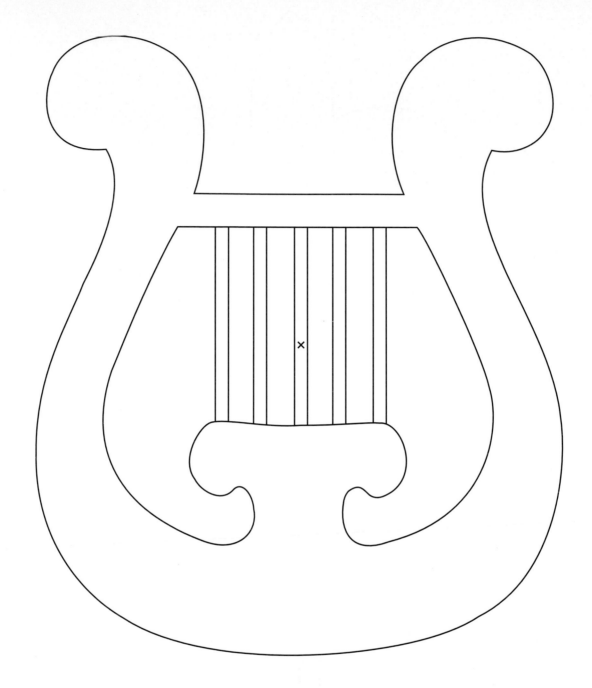

LYRE

Lyre — #7, page 37, padded
Strings — #2, page 32, corded with full
  interlining

LAUREL WREATH

Wreath — #3, page 33, corded curve
Leaves — #7, page 37, padded

CHERRY WREATH

Wreath — #3, page 33, corded curve
Cherry stems — #5, page 35, branching
  stems
Cherries and leaves — #7, page 37, padded

ANITA SHACKELFORD: SURFACE TEXTURES

TEAR DROP
FLOWER

Stems — #2, page 32, corded with full
  interlining
Petals — #16, page 46, stuffed

Leaf and Berries

Leaf — #9, page 39, padded with open center
  channel
Vein lines — #8, page 38, quilted through all
  layers
Berries — #16, page 46, stuffed

PINEAPPLE

Fruit — #6, page 36, crossed channels
Fruit sections — #19, page 49, stuffed
  and tacked
Leaf and cartouche — #7, page 37,
  padded

FLOWER AND
BERRIES

Stems and berries full interlining for #2,
  page 32, corded stems and berries,
  #16, page 46 for stuffing technique
Flower — #8, page 38, padded with interior lines quilted through all layers

GRAPES

Stems and grapes, full interlining for
  # 2, page 32, corded stems,
   #3, page 33, for corded tendrils
#16, page 46, stuffed grapes
Leaf — #8, page 38, padded with interi-
  or lines quilted through all layers

SUNFLOWERS

Flower petals — #16, page 47, stuffed
Leaves — #8, page 38, padded with interior lines quilted through all layers
Stems — #2, page 32, corded with full interlining

QUEEN ANNE'S LACE

Flowers with full interlining for #2, page
   32, corded channels and #16, page 46,
   stuffed tops
Stems — #1, page 31, corded channels
Leaves — #7, page 37, padded

MARGUERITES

Flower centers — #3, page 33, corded curves
Petals — #16, page 46, stuffed
Stems — #1, page 31, corded channels
Leaves — #8, page 38, padded with interior
  lines quilted through all layers

JACOBEAN

Large leaf — #8, page 38, padded with
   interior lines quilted through all layers
Flower — #8, page 38
Berry cap — #7, page 37, padded
Berries — #16, page 46, stuffed
Stems — #1, page 31, corded channels
Small leaf — #7, page 37

WILDFLOWERS

Flowers — #3, page 33, corded curves
Petals — #7, page 37, padded
Berries — #16, page 46, stuffed
Stems — #1, page 31, corded channels
Leaves — #10, page 40, padded and sur-
   face quilted

BIRD AND FLOWERS

Flowers — #16, page 46, stuffed
Leaves — #10, page 40, padded with surface quilting
Bird — #8, page 38, padded with interior lines quilted through all layers
Stems — #1, page 31, corded channels

LADY SLIPPER

Top Loop — #3, page 33, corded curves
Center — #16, page 46, stuffed
Petals — #7, page 37, padded
Stems — #1, page 31, corded channels
Leaves — #8, page 38, padded with inte-
  rior lines quilted through

ANITA SHACKELFORD: SURFACE TEXTURES

PEONY

Flowers — #19, page 49, stuffed and
tacked through all layers
Stems — #1, page 31, corded channels
Leaves — #8, page 38, padded with interior lines quilted through all layers

ROSE

Flowers — #19, page 49, stuffed and
   tacked through all layers
Small leaves — #7, page 37, padded
Medium leaf — #8, page 38, padded with
   interior lines quilted through all layers
Stems — #1, page 31, corded channels
Large leaf — #11, page 41, corded and
   padded

FEATHERED HEART

Feathers — #23, page 53, single, with
  corded spine
Circle — #16, page 46, stuffed

FEATHERED PINEAPPLE

Feathers — #23, page 53, single, with
corded spine
Cross bar — #1, page 31, corded channel
Circles — #16, page 46, stuffed

LEAF AND FEATHER WREATH

#24, page 54, padded with interior lines
quilted through all layers

FEATHER WREATH

#3, page 33, corded curve
Feathers — #25, page 55, isolated feathers, stuffed, or padded

ANITA SHACKELFORD: SURFACE TEXTURES

FEATHER PLUME

#22, page 52, Fiddlehead feather

I used several different styles of stipple quilting when I finished my sampler quilt "Through Rose Colored Glasses." Compare the notes and illustrations here to the photos of the finished piece to see how the various stipple patterns complement the main motif in each block.

Line Stipple on the Diagonal

Echo Stipple

Random Stipple

Line Stipple

Grid Stipple

Echo Stipple

Echo Stipple inside, Random Stipple background

Random Stipple background

Rosette Stipple

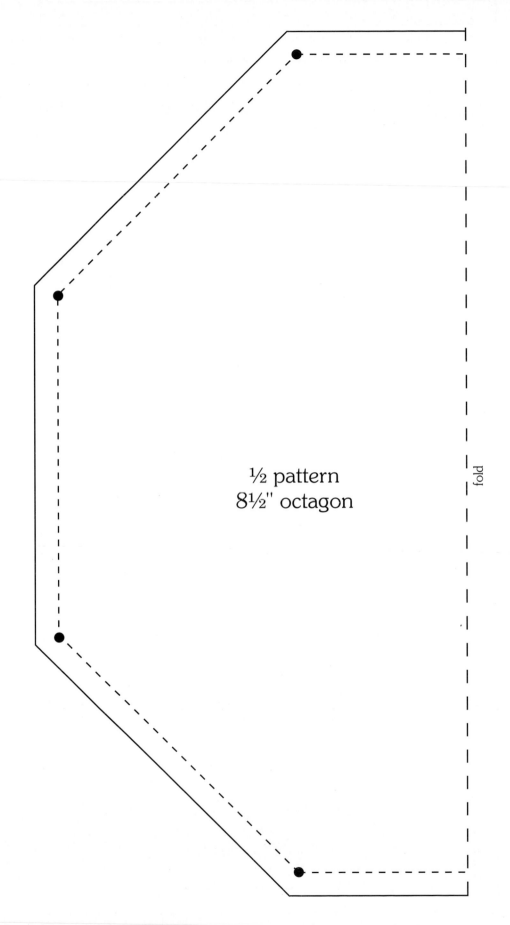

½ pattern
8½" octagon

fold

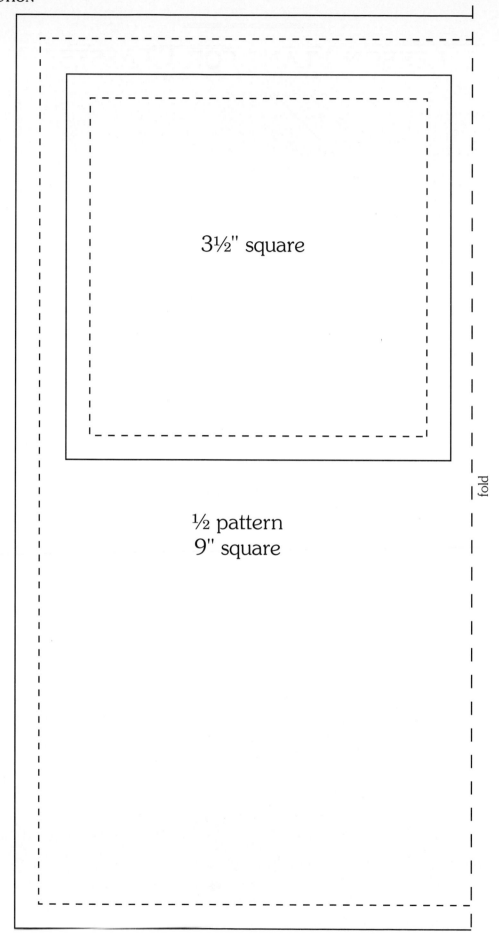

3½" square

½ pattern
9" square

fold

LESSON PLANS FOR CLASSES

For instructors or shop owners wishing to develop workshops based on the information and patterns in this book, I encourage you to do so. Below are several suggested lesson plans which will fit a variety of schedules and skill levels. Use the book and these classes to help your students add beautiful surface textures to their quilts. Enjoy!

1 Class:
Choose a beautiful, large scale print fabric for 8"–9" blocks and a trapunto design to complement the mood of the print. Teach raised work in class.

2 Classes:
1. Make a patchwork block in 8"–10" size.
2. Teach raised work techniques for alternate block.

6 Classes:
For students who want a quick overview of the many raised work techniques. Work through a series of small technique blocks.

1. Corded — flower stem, branching cherry stems
2. Corded with full interlining — rings, tear drop flower
3. Padded — little flower, oak leaf
4. Stuffed — sunflower
5. Stuffed in units — rosebud
6. Feathers — feather with interior lines quilted to batiste

Miniature Quilts in 2 classes:

1. Paper pieced block in 3" or 4" size.
2. Small raised work technique for alternate block.

1. Mark whole cloth pattern and begin raised work.
2. Begin background quilting with line, grid, or stipple patterns.
12 Months:

For those interested in an in-depth study of the techniques and the larger patterns. One class will teach technique on a small block and the following class will focus on the corresponding large pattern. Suggested patterns are listed here by skill level — Easy (E), Intermediate (I), Advanced (A).

1. Corded — flower stem, branching cherry stems
   (E) Tulips
   (I) Flower and Berries
   (A) Fern

2. Corded with full interlining — rings, tear drop flower
   (E) Laurel and Cherry Wreaths
   (I) Grapes
   (A) Queen Anne's Lace

3. Padded — little flower, oak leaf
   (E) Oak Leaves, Tulips
   (I) Cherries and Laurel Leaves
   (A) Jacobean

4. Stuffed — sunflower
   (E) Flower and Berries, Grapes
   (I) Sunflowers, Bird and Flowers
   (A) Marguerites

5. Stuffed in units — rosebud
   (A) Peony, Rose

6. Feathers — feather with interior lines quilted
   (I) Feathered Plume
   (A) Feathered Heart, Feathered Pineapple

BIBLIOGRAPHY

Allen, Gloria Seaman, and Nancy Gibson Tuckhorn. *A Maryland Album: Quiltmaking Traditions ~ 1634-1934*. Rutledge Hill Press Nashville, TN, 1995.

Berenson, Kathryn. *Quilts of Provence*. Henry Holt, Inc., New York, and Thames and Hudson, London, 1996.

Berenson, Kathryn. *Origins and Traditions of Marseilles Needlework, Uncoverings 1995, Volume 16* of the Research Papers of the American Quilt Study Group.

Bishop, Robert. *New Discoveries in American Quilts*. E.P. Dutton, New York, 1975.

Bowman, Doris M. *The Smithsonian Treasury American Quilts*. Smithsonian Institution Press, Washington, DC, 1991.

Brackman, Barbara. *Clues in the Calico: A Guide to Identifying and Dating Antique Quilts*. EPM Publications, Alexandria, Virginia, 1989.

Clark, Ricky, George W. Knepper and Ellice Ronsheim. *Quilts in Community*. Rutledge Hill Press, Nashville, TN, 1991.

Clark, Ricky. *Quilted Gardens*. Rutledge Hill Press, Nashville, TN, 1994.

Colby, Averil. *Quilting*. Charles Schribner's Sons, New York, NY, 1971.

Dunton, Dr. William Rush, Jr. *Old Quilts*. Baltimore, MD, 1946.

Garoutte, Sally. *Marseilles Quilts and Their Woven Offspring Uncoverings 1982, Volume 3* of the research papers of the American Quilt Study Group.

Goldsborough, Jennifer F. *An Album of Baltimore Album Quilt Studies Uncoverings 1994, Volume 15* of the Research Papers of the American Quilt Study Group.

Goldsborough, Jennifer F. *Lavish Legacies. Baltimore Album and Related Quilts in the Collection of the Maryland Historical Society*. MHS, Baltimore, MD, 1994.

Hall, Carrie and Rose Kretsinger. *The Romance of the Patchwork Quilt*. Crown Publishers, Inc., 1935.

Hornback, Nancy. *Quilts in Red and Green: The Flowering of Folk Design in 19th Century America*. Exhibit catalog, The Wichita/Sedgwick County Historical Museum, Wichita, Kansas, 1992.

Kiracofe, Roderick with Mary Elizabeth Johnson. *The American Quilt: A History of Cloth and Comfort 1750-1950*. Clarkson Potter, New York, 1993.

Marston, Gwen and Joe Cunningham. *Quilting with Style: Principles for Great Pattern Design*. American Quilter's Society, Paducah, KY, 1993.

Miller, Phyllis D. *Encyclopedia of Designs for Quilting*. American Quilter's Society, Paducah, KY, 1996.

Morris, Patricia J. *The Ins & Outs: Perfecting the Quilting Stitch*. American Quilter's Society, Paducah, KY, 1990.

Orlofsky, Patsy and Myron. *Quilts in America*. McGraw-Hill, 1974, Abbeville Press, Inc., New York, 1992.

Nelson, Cyril I. and Carter Houck. *Treasury of American Quilts*. Crown Publishers, New York, 1982.

Orr, Anne. "Quilt Today," *Better Homes & Gardens*, February 1943, pp. 46-47.

Ramsey, Bets and Merikay Waldvogel. *Quilts of Tennessee: Images of Domestic Life Prior to 1930*. Rutledge Hill Press, Nashville, TN, 1986.

Safford, Carleton L. and Robert Bishop. *America's Quilts and Coverlets*. E.P. Dutton, New York, 1972.

Shackelford, Anita. *Three Dimensional Appliqué and Embroidery Embellishment: Techniques for Today's Album Quilt*. American Quilter's Society, Paducah, KY, 1994.

Wagner, Debra. *Teach Yourself Machine Piecing & Quilting*. Chilton Book Company, Radnor, PA, 1992.

Waldvogel, Merikay and Barbara Brackman. *Patchwork Souvenirs of the 1933 World's Fair*. Rutledge Hill Press, Nashville, TN, 1993.

Walner, Hari. *Trapunto by Machine*. C&T Publishing, Lafayette, CA, 1996.

ABOUT THE AUTHOR

Anita Shackelford is probably best known for her album quilts which combine original, personalized designs with nineteenth century dimensional appliqué techniques. Her first book, *Three Dimensional Appliqué and Embroidery Embellishment: Techniques for Today's Album Quilt* was published by the American Quilter's Society in 1994. She is also the designer of the RucheMark™ ruching guides. Anita enjoys working in a variety of styles and techniques in her own quilts. This book reflects her interest in raised work and her passion for fine hand quilting.

An award winning quiltmaker, with ten Best of Show awards and many others for technical excellence, she is currently the only quiltmaker to have twice won the National Quilting Association's Mary Krickbaum Award for Excellence in Hand Quilting.

In addition to making quilts and writing about quiltmaking, Anita spends much of her time lecturing and teaching for shops and guilds across the country. Her work has been published in *American Quilter, American Patchwork & Quilting, Better Homes & Gardens' Fashion Ideas, Quilter's Newsletter Magazine, Quilting Today, Quilt Craft, Quilting International, Traditional Quilter, Patchwork Quilt Tsushin, Americana Magazine,* and *Award Winning Quilts & Their Makers, Vol. I.* She has been making quilts since 1967 and teaching since 1980.

Anita lives in Bucyrus, Ohio, with her husband Richard. Their family also includes two daughters, Jennifer and Elisa, a son-in-law Scott, and two grandchildren, Amber and Brandon.

AQS BOOKS ON QUILTS

This is only a partial listing of the books on quilts that are available from the American Quilter's Society. AQS books are known the world over for their timely topics, clear writing, beautiful color photographs, and accurate illustrations and patterns. Most of the following books are available from your local bookseller, quilt shop, or public library. If you are unable to locate certain titles in your area, you may order by mail from the AMERICAN QUILTER'S SOCIETY, P.O. Box 3290, Paducah, KY 42002-3290. Customers with Visa or MasterCard may phone in orders from 7:00–5:00 CST, Monday–Friday, Toll Free 1-800-626-5420. Add $2.00 for postage for the first book ordered and $0.40 for each additional book. Include item number, title, and price when ordering. Allow 14 to 21 days for delivery.